"*When the Soul Surr*[enders] hits the reader to the core emotionally and spiritually. It is an easy read that keeps you wanting to learn more."

SELENA HELVEY

"*When the Soul Surrenders* helps you to search your soul and find God's amazing love and healing."

LANEY WEBER, Ph.D.
Director of Operations, BioScience Writers, Houston, TX

"This book shows that whatever has assaulted our hearts, our souls, God is in control and loves us—a must read!"

SHELLEY GABEL
Marketing Manager, DTJ Design

"You (Andrea) reach to the inner core, where all of us need to be reached."

MARY KELLY

"Be prepared to be bathed in the love of God as you read this book. Andrea has such an amazing grasp of the human soul and a knowledge of what a damaged soul needs. As she describes the lessons learned from Andy's journey, your own soul will be gently massaged back to life."

PATRICIA JUSTER
Tikkun International Ministries

"Andrea's heart-warming words will refresh anyone's parched soul. In this book she offers new insights on how to truly surrender to God and find strength, peace, and purpose in this journey called life."

JEAN BLACKMER
Author of
Boy-sterous Living: Celebrating Your Loud and Rowdy Life with Sons,
and Publishing Manager for MOPS International.

WHEN THE *Soul* SURRENDERS

WHEN THE *Soul* SURRENDERS

*Allowing the beauty
of God's work
to be displayed in your life*

ANDREA LEE BINDER

*Discover
Abundant Life*
PUBLISHING

When the Soul Surrenders
Allowing the beauty of God's work to be displayed in your life

Copyright © 2009 Andrea Lee Binder

All rights reserved.

No part of this book, except for brief passages for purposes of review, may be duplicated or reproduced in any form or by any electronic or mechanical means, without permission in writing from the publisher.

PUBLISHED BY
Discover Abundant Life Publishing
www.discoverabundantlife.com

PRODUCED BY
Boulder Bookworks, Boulder, Colorado USA
www.boulderbookworks.com

FRONT COVER ART: "Dancing in Thin Air" by Blair Anderson
BACK COVER PHOTO: David Page, DMPage Images
www.dmpageimages.com
COVER DESIGN: Luke Flowers, Luke Flowers Design
www.lukeflowers.com

First Edition

ISBN: 978-0-9840835-0-3

Printed in the United States of America

DEDICATION

I dedicate this book to
all the little "Andys" in the world.

*May the work of God
be displayed in and through
their lives.*

Contents

ACKNOWLEDGMENTS 11

INTRODUCTION A Taste of Heaven 13

CHAPTER ONE In the Beginning 18
When the unloved soul surrenders,
love is found.
GOING FURTHER IN SURRENDER 29

CHAPTER TWO Thou Art With Me 30
When the lonely soul surrenders,
belonging is established.
GOING FURTHER IN SURRENDER 39

CHAPTER THREE Poor in Spirit 40
When the humble soul surrenders,
riches are realized.
GOING FURTHER IN SURRENDER 49

CHAPTER FOUR A Guided Tour 50
When the wayward soul surrenders,
guidance is given.
GOING FURTHER IN SURRENDER 58

CHAPTER FIVE Suffering Sojourner 59
When the pained soul surrenders,
power is displayed.
GOING FURTHER IN SURRENDER 69

CHAPTER SIX — A Quenchless Thirst.............................. 70
When the dehydrated soul surrenders,
living water flows.
GOING FURTHER IN SURRENDER 77

CHAPTER SEVEN — Life Is Messy..................................... 78
When the sinful soul surrenders,
forgiveness and freedom are enjoyed.
GOING FURTHER IN SURRENDER 82

CHAPTER EIGHT — His Glory Manifested.......................... 83
When the faithful soul surrenders,
God is glorified.
GOING FURTHER IN SURRENDER 90

REFERENCES 91

ACKNOWLEDGMENTS

I must take a moment to thank my "dream" team of readers. I could have done it without them, but I probably wouldn't have. I thank my long time California friend, Dale Arnesen, who is a quick draw with the highlighter button. I believe her help, prayers, and persistent correction have taught me to be a better writer. My beautiful friend in Colorado, Manon Crespi; without her cheerleading, I might have quit this project a long time ago. Manon has the gift of encouragement. She made me believe in the value of this story. Stephen Olsen, my brother-in-Christ, favorite theologian and best friend living in the Czech Republic, whom I sent my first few chapters to in fear and trembling. He sent them back full of grace. Stephen challenged me to rethink the Bible "truths" I seemed to just make up. I would also like to thank Jean Blackmer, the most famous and wonderful writer I know. If it weren't for all her editing, my book would be 1000 pages long. She has inspired me with her own giftedness and gentleness. To my colleague and friend, Paul Townsend, in appreciation of his prayers and support even while he struggled with cancer. I especially thank my husband and best friend, Gene Binder. I love you forever. I thank you for making the computer work, for spurring me on and for making me feel beautiful.

I am grateful for these people who recently joined my team to make my book come alive—Blair Anderson, Alan Bernhard, Luke Flowers, Liz Gravagne, Michelle Myers, and Alan Stark.

And finally, Jesus, who surrendered his life for me and who is teaching me how to surrender my life for him... I love you Abba. I pray that the words on these pages and the meditations of our hearts will be more than pleasing to you.

INTRODUCTION

A Taste of Heaven

ONE OF MY FAVORITE AVOCATIONS is to encounter times of solitude. I love it. I crave it. And I also avoid it. I have two special places in Colorado that summon me to come, be still, and discover that God is God. One is a friend's cabin in Winter Park. Here, in the immeasurable forest situated within the range of the Rocky Mountains, sits a lovely lodge that greets me like a long lost friend. The other sanctuary is the Abby in Virginia Dale. As I am driving to this cloister of Benedictine nuns, whose "soul" mission is to spend several hours each day in prayer, I am overwhelmed by the beauty of the gently rolling hills, artistically mixed in with coppery-colored rock formations. The beautiful landscape seems to stretch on forever.

I haven't always had beautiful sanctuaries to retreat to. Often, especially when my children were younger, I would find a quiet corner in the local library. Or, I would go to the local Catholic church and sit in the stillness, listening to God. For most of my Christian life, I have desired to get away from it all, alone, and to be quiet before the Lord. When I actually do, although it is difficult to pull myself away from day-to-day "all-important" life, I am richly blessed. In many ways, I find that solitude feels as if I have finally entered into the land promised to the Israelites: "a land flowing with milk and honey" (Exod. 3:8*). During these times, I feel like I get to have a taste of heaven.

---

* Bible verses are taken from the New International Version unless otherwise noted.

Perhaps a corner in your favorite coffee shop becomes your very own heavenly place of solitude, your promised land. It doesn't matter where; what is important is that you have a sacred place and time where your soul can surrender. At these moments, the soul can breathe deeply and then be still before the Lord. Ultimately, it only matters that you make a place in your life where you are free to enter into the Lord's presence.

David the Psalmist said it this way: "Be still, and know that I am God" (Ps. 46:10). Although I long for this sacred time with God, I have to tell you it is one of the most difficult things for me to do. Most of us do not take to stillness, quiet, and surrender naturally. Our souls long for it, but part of us—that still, quiet voice of our inner being—has difficulty being heard.

I compare this opposition to surrender felt by many adults to a child who doesn't want to stop playing and get into the bathtub. To the child, the prospect of taking a bath can seem like a big, wet pleasure-robber. I can remember my own mother calling to me and saying, "Andrea, it's time for your bath." Immediately I would start complaining: "I don't want to take a bath. I am not even dirty—look." But, once I surrendered to the tub of hot water, slid in and embraced the bubbles, I couldn't imagine ever getting out. My mother could not get me out of the tub.

Soul surrender is very similar. We resist it until we experience it. Metaphorically speaking, it is like getting into a warm bath and soaking in all that the God of the universe has for us. God desires for us to use this opportunity to let go of every ache and pain. This time of discovery is like a mountaintop experience, and, at the same time, can even be a glory-filled desert. We learn through surrender that God is present not only on a glorious mountaintop, but also in the barren desert. Surrender is a glorious moment in time when we feel welcomed into the Lord's presence.

Here is the point: how can we experience God if we won't enter the "bath" of surrender? Just as a child collects dirt day-by-day or moment-by-moment, depending on the child, adults collect pains from the past, worries about the present, and fears about the future. There is only one way for that child to get clean: she must take a bath. So, finding time to be still with God is like taking a long, hot bubble bath. A five-minute bath will not be enough; it must be a long soak, until every fiber of your being has wrinkled up like an accordion of flesh.

The opposite is more often true: we run from God. Unless you are a monk, a nun, or someone like Mother Teresa, I am certain that, like me, you have every reason to avoid time with God.

When I became a Christian, I was taught that a twenty-minute quiet time was the daily discipline needed to experience God's presence. I am not speaking about a twenty-minute quiet time here. For most people, even that is hard. But I am talking about more than that. Specifically, I mean a time with God when you willingly submit yourself before his presence. You don't watch the clock. You don't check off your daily prayer requests. You simply offer him your deepest authentic self, open and truthful. Surrendered. In this moment, you are able to sing the hymn "I Surrender All" with all of your heart, soul, mind, and strength.

If I were to sum up our generation and culture with one word, it would be *distracted.* We are so distracted with life that the idea of being still and knowing that God is God is almost laughable.

Many of my friends have laughed at me about my "need" to be with God for an extended time. (I think seven days of solitude has been my longest, so far). I don't think they are making fun of me, and I don't take it personally. I think that when the idea of spending extended time with God is mentioned, it stirs up fear, insecurity, or maybe guilt. I am sure it must appear somewhat "godly." Please don't think that my idea of soul surrender is only for saints. It is for everyone. I am merely a sojourner, learning to surrender my all to God, hoping to encourage you on your own journey.

As I was saying, we are distracted people, living in a distracted culture. We are running around in many directions, living life. Some years ago, I read a book titled *Little House on the Freeway* (Kimmel 1990). I believe the title aptly depicts the American dream. Or perhaps I should say the American reality, because, as dreams go, it leaves something to be desired.

Sometimes, if we feel like it, we fit God into our frantic schedules. We especially love our American churches, because we can get in, get out, and get on with our lives.

At our church in Boulder, Colorado, we are considered to have a long worship time. We often worship by singing for about forty minutes. Some churches have had to cut down on the time for worship to rush people out of the first service and get more people in for the next service. Maybe you have experienced this. It often can feel more like bumper-to-bumper traffic than an experience in God's presence. Yet, we so often accept that our Sunday morning experiences should fill up all the needs of our souls. Honestly, do you believe that if you put in an hour on Sunday morning that you have truly experienced God?

On the other hand, you may be scratching your head and asking yourself, "Why must I surrender?" Or, "What exactly is soul surrender?" Simply put, it is the letting go of self, for filling by God. Charles Allen, in his 1997 book *God's Psychiatry*, says "We are created incomplete and we cannot be at rest until there's a satisfaction of our deepest hunger ... the yearning of our souls."

Soul surrender offers you an opportunity to experience the presence of the Lord. Each and every time we surrender our souls (a letting go of self for a filling by God), we experience his presence. When the soul surrenders, a delicious taste of heaven can be experienced. Just as the Psalm writer David said, "Taste and see that the Lord is good" (Ps. 34:8).

Throughout this book, I will weave the story of one of my first clients. I will call her "Andy." I have included a Bible study called "Going Further in Surrender" that can be used for individual study or as a group study.

I hope you enjoy the story about Andy, and approach it as if you were reading an interesting novel. I hope the Bible study will guide you to go further in your own journey of surrender. He is waiting for you.

CHAPTER ONE

In the Beginning

When the unloved soul surrenders,
love is found.

"God is love."

(1 John 4:16b)

Andy was the second child of a young family living near
Venice Beach, California in the 1950s. Her teenage parents
struggled to get by. Her dad was a tree surgeon, and her mother
a cocktail waitress. When they were not working, they were
fighting. I remember Andy saying, "In a way, they were just kids
raising kids."

Andy experienced abuse in many different forms (emotional,
psychological, physical, and sexual) but, for her, it was the
physical abuse and violence that had the most horrific effect
on her life. She understood the profound impact this kind of
violence would have on her life. At times, she felt destined to live
out her painful childhood in a never-ending journey of grief and
fear, filled with a sense of helplessness. I asked her to tell me
about her childhood.

I must have been about five or six when we moved from Venice Beach to the San Fernando Valley in California. I had the best—and only—tree swing in the neighborhood. Everyone on the block came over to my yard to swing. The big boys liked to mimic a Herculean stance on top of the huge cinder block wall; they would swing out yodeling the Tarzan call. I didn't need to do any fancy flying acrobatics; I just loved to swing back and forth, higher and higher, the rhythm swaying me into a peaceful meditation, like a sailboat rocking on the swells of a calm blue sea. As I pumped higher and higher, my toes could almost touch the leaves that were tap-dancing to the song of the breeze.

Every so often, my dad would rig up a new seat for me. I had a Goodyear tire seat, a turquoise bucket seat, a standard wood board seat, and, of course, there was always the basic rope loop seat. The eternal oak tree became my best friend. My back yard on Sylvia Street was my Garden of Eden. I felt happy, safe, and free.

On Easter Saturday, my mom bought me a fancy dress; you know—one of those crisp satin dresses from a cheap department store. She purchased an array of accessories to go with the dress: white patent-leather shoes that looked like a freshly peeled hard-boiled egg; soft white socks with a bit of lace trim around the cuffs; and an ornamental, pearly purse.

I was Cinderella off to the ball. I was picture perfect. I didn't mind my despicable brother calling me freckle face. I didn't notice the reflection in the mirror. I saw radiant beauty: deep blue eyes, a nose the size of a rose bud; and hair shining like the San Fernando Valley sun on a clear day.

"Will my daddy think I am pretty?" I wondered. I could hear his closest friend talking on and on in the holy of holies—the living room; the place the king worshipped his idol. I pranced and trailed out like a trail of cigarette smoke into the dark chamber.

Boldly standing in front of the sacred box—the television set—I held my dress out like a girl ready to do-si-do with her beau at the Friday night square dance. "Look at me, Daddy, do you think I am pretty?" I whispered. Time stood still, and, for just a moment, I fantasized that the king stood up and said, "May I have this dance?" The king took me in his arms and swirled me as he smiled like a proud groom dancing with his bride.

The sweet dream erupted into a nightmare. It was as if I had been awakened from a peaceful sleep to the rumbling of a California earthquake. The rumbling jarred me into reality. I was wide awake, and trapped in the middle of his furious response. My daddy purged himself in a fit of rage.

My brother grabbed me. We barely escaped what felt like the pull of the earth opening up. My daddy smashed everything in sight while yelling obscenities at my brother and me. We ran fast, through the back gate of the yard into the alley. I tried to hide the virgin white trim of my satin dress as we stooped behind the metal armored garbage cans. The smell of the trash penetrated the delicate fabric of my pounding heart. A voice spoke to me from someplace dark, saying, "You're not pretty. You're not beautiful. Your daddy doesn't love you. You will never be loved."

It seemed like a very long time passed, as long as a kid waits for school to end and summer vacation to start, but eventually a car—the black bomb as we called it—approached our fortress like a savior. In a disgusted tone, Mom simply said, "Get in!"

My best friend—the oak, greeted me like a rained

out welcome home parade for a hero. I rocked myself back and forth, seeking to comfort my battered, unloved soul.

It's strange, but somehow, all of a sudden, I knew something about life that I didn't want to know (like Eve did in the garden when she ate the apple from the tree of good and evil): Life is very painful. Life is not pretty. Shiny satin fabric, patent leather shoes, and even new socks would not mask the dark emptiness of my sad and unloved soul.

A few months later, we moved to an apartment building. I missed my tree, my swing. I missed my own pretend Garden of Eden.

When Andy stood before her dad and said, "Look at me, Daddy, do you think I am pretty?" She was really asking, "Do you love me, Daddy?"

Everyone, from the beginning of time, has asked this question. Some of us get this all-important question answered with resounding affirmation and acceptance. Some get the question answered in the form of rejection. Think for a moment about your own childhood. When you asked the question, "Am I loved?" were you accepted or rejected? Were you hugged or hit? Were you affirmed or abused or ignored? Were you unconditionally loved and cherished, or was the love and adoration you craved unattainable? Every person has a story that revolves around the question, "Am I loved?"

On the journey of surrender, we are introduced to the God of love. We will struggle to feel his love. Some will so adamantly oppose the journey that they will choose instead to live out life in a fortified city of self. In so doing, they have answered the question for themselves. They have concluded, "No, I am not loved."

If you come to this conclusion, you might feel safe. You are self-guarded, and believe that you do not need love. You have decided that you, alone, are enough. This is a narrow, sad existence.

Look around you and you will see self-guarded, unloved people everywhere. Perhaps you don't have to look far. It is difficult to comprehend the choices people make. For example, the unshaven, bent-over homeless man I see daily at the off-ramp, collecting money because he needs bus fare to go somewhere. He is searching for something or someone. He is struggling for something, when, all along, the God of love has offered him a safe refuge for his unloved soul.

You don't have to be a homeless person to feel unloved. You can be anyone—a mother, a father, or even a beautiful little child—and feel unloved. You can be surrounded by a multitude of family members and friends, and feel unloved. You can be a top executive making lots of money, or a housewife and mother, and feel unloved.

We were not created to search for love. We were created to receive God's love. Let's meet the God of love.

The first chapter of the book of Genesis tells us that in the beginning, our loving Father created a wonderful environment for his children to enjoy. You might say he was preparing for the arrival of his first child. He wanted to communicate the depth of his love.

"In the beginning God created the heavens and the earth" (Gen. 1:1). Have you ever wondered why? Why would God do this? The Bible says "Now the earth was formless and empty, darkness was over the surface of the deep, and the Spirit of God was hovering over the waters" (Gen. 1:2).

The spirit of God was "hovering." I love that word, *hovering.* I picture a loving parent hovering over his newborn child.

The very first thing that God created was light. He said, "Let there be light" (Gen. 1:3). It is interesting to think about why God would create light first. I can only speculate, but perhaps he wanted to see his creation, and he knew that his creation would need light for survival.

Apparently, the earth was not only formless and empty; it was completely covered with water. The next day, God separated the waters. He made the sky separate from the water (Gen. 1:6–7).

Then he made dry ground (Gen. 1:9). He must have known that he would be creating creatures not just for the water, but also for the land. God is so smart! Not only would there be dry ground to walk on, but there would be rich soil, which would produce seed-bearing crops for food. Later, the land would also provide a sense of significance for man, as he cultivated it, and security for man, because he would have plenty to eat.

Next, God created seasons and time (Gen. 1:14). He knew that his creation would need a sense of order, and that order would promote a sense of security. He is like the author of a good love story, weaving an intricate account for all of eternity.

God had everything set up beautifully, as if he were preparing for the guest of honor to appear. He created light, sky, land, seasons and time. He could now create living things, and then, he created man. God created male and female, and he blessed them (Gen. 1:24–28).

The creation story reminds me of the time when I was pregnant with my first child. We created a bright, beautiful nursery for our child. We wanted our child to have a place of belonging. We wanted the environment to be safe and secure. We desired that our child would see the beautiful preparations, and thus would know her significance. We loved her and prepared for her, even though we had not met her yet. Our hearts were bursting with love as we awaited the arrival of our first child.

I imagine that God marveled at his own creation as I read, "Thus the heavens and earth were completed in all their vast array" (Gen. 2:1).

Adam and Eve didn't have to ask, "Are we loved?" They knew to the depth of their souls that the very nature of God is love. He provided for all their needs and placed them into a perfect environment. They experienced complete freedom in God's presence and with one another. They loved the responsibility of caring for the garden. They had authority over the birds, fish, and animals. What fun they must have experienced!

Every day they had two chores: to rule and to reproduce. Their lives were uncomplicated. They were free. They were loved without question.

We know that God gave Adam direction for life. As Adam enjoyed the splendors of the garden, God said, "You are free to eat from any tree in the garden" (Gen. 2:16). That was what Adam could do. Then he said, "but you must not eat from the tree of the knowledge of good and evil, for when you eat of it you will surely die" (Gen. 2:17). Can you imagine what it was like for Adam and Eve to be given access to everything that God had created except for the fruit from one little tree?

I recently attended a wedding at which my husband offici-ated. I noticed the cake at the reception. It was beautifully displayed, with layer upon layer of luscious cream frosting. If that were the end of it, I wouldn't even bother to go on with the story, but here was my dilemma: the cake and the table were adorned with fruit. Not just fruit, but cherries. I saw juicy, succulent, Bing cherries. Before the cake was cut, I was com-pelled to taste, and see that the cherries were good. I would walk by the cake table and steal a cherry or two. Then I would go outside to hide from the guests so that they couldn't see me spitting out the pits. I just couldn't seem to help myself. I gave a cherry to my husband, and he ate one, too.

I empathize with Eve's temptation, and I understand why she would eat the fruit from the tree of the knowledge of good and evil. At this point in history, the woman and man made the choice to disobey God. The Christian faith calls this time "the fall of man."

Something dark entered into this perfect world—sin. When sin entered, paradise was lost. A struggle began. Love was ruined.

When Adam and Eve bit into the succulent fruit, suddenly

their eyes were opened. Like deer caught in the headlights of an oncoming truck, they were exposed. Immediately they grabbed some fig leaves, and hid their nakedness. They were filled with awkwardness. They didn't even know what to call this new feeling. Today, we call it shame. In their shame, they hid from God (Gen. 3:6–8). At this time, innocent, unquestioning love was lost.

Despite living in a fallen world, sometimes I am given a glimpse of what life in the garden might have been like. Our little granddaughter lived with us until she was almost two years old. Her favorite time of the day was "nakey time." Just before her bath, she would get naked and run around the house announcing to us that it was nakey time. She felt no need to hide her nakedness. In her "nakey time" of play, she boldly proclaimed, "I am loved—every bit of me!"

Once sin entered into the garden, Adam and Eve lost their innocence. Their sense of uninhibited belonging, to each other and to God, dissipated. Their shame forced them to hide. For the first time, fear engulfed God's children, and their sense of security vanished. The questions began.

As God questioned his children about what happened, they began blaming one another for the offense. Like kids caught with cookie crumbs all over their faces, they turned to one another, dumbfounded, pointing their fingers and saying, "he made me do it." Thus, blame became the post-fall method of communication.

Adam blames God for giving him "that" woman; Eve blames Satan (Gen. 3:12–13). Satan, well, I imagine he would have kicked the dog, if there had been a dog around to kick. Instead, he slithered away with a grin on his face.

For the first time, sin had entered into this perfect world. Love was no longer sacred, but tarnished, polluted. Innocent love was lost.

Finally, there were consequences for the sin committed. God gives Adam work to do. He calls it "painful toil" (Gen. 3:17). Up to this point, Adam had never experienced anything painful. He would have to learn to work the ground and deal with thorns and weeds. For the first time, he would sweat (Gen. 3:19).

For Eve, there were consequences such as pain in childbirth. Her ultimate desire would be for her husband's love and his rule over her (Gen. 3:16). Although Eve once had her focus in perfect order, she would now have to grapple for her sense of belonging, security, and significance. She would be like a teenager holding a yellow daisy. In wonder, she would pull off a petal and say, "He loves me" and then another petal, "He loves me not." Adam and Eve were stuck with the pervasive question: "Am I loved?"

God, in his tender mercy and his love, clothed his disobedient children and sent them out of the garden (Gen. 3:21–23). You might say that God grounds Adam and Eve from the garden and adopts a tough-love approach with his rebellious teens.

The creation story is especially important, because it relates to the journey of surrender. Like Adam and Eve, we are made in the image of God, with a yearning to be loved.

It is through a personal sense of belonging, security and significance to God and one another that we experience love. These are God-given needs. They are legitimate longings of the soul, causing each person to yearn especially for God's love. These longings are the soul's attempt to seek out God the Father and ask, "Do you love me?"

Because of the fall, Adam and Eve had to experience a laborious life. They struggled to feel love. They could not go back to the past, to the garden life as they knew it before sin entered in. Since that time, we have all craved the pre-fall state of the garden. We want it back. We want to go back to the garden before the fall. We want innocence. We want paradise. We search for Utopia. We want a permanent vacation, a place where we can run naked on the beach. We travel, and grab anything that somehow represents the pre-fall state of the Garden of Eden, when love was pure.

Allender and Longman, authors of *Intimate Allies* (1999), say this about the post-fall desire of the human soul: "Our souls are wired for what we will never enjoy until Eden is restored in the new heaven and earth. We are built with a distant memory of Eden."

Just as the creation story is fundamental for the journey of life, understanding the outcome of the fall is essential for the journey of soul surrender. This might sound simple, but the bottom line of the fall of man is twofold. Men and women will struggle for love:

- man will look for belonging, security and significance from his work; and

- woman will look for belonging, security and significance from her man.

We must understand that the loving God creates us with souls that are desperately wired for belonging, security and significance. We have longings to find fulfillment in God's love. What we really need is God. Instead, man will look to his work and woman will look to her man to meet these longings, believing they have found the real deal.

So, we have the current condition of life. Basically, we are a bunch of unloved souls searching for love. We seek a love fulfillment through work or through another person, when the God of our universe stands patiently waiting for us to come to him.

As children, we deeply desire the love of our earthly fathers. In adolescence, we continue struggling for Daddy's love, along with the love and adoration of our peers. In our young adult years, we look to the opposite sex to fulfill our love longings. Later in life we often think, "Will I ever be loved?"

When we understand that we are struggling for love, we can then take the next step on the journey of surrender. In this place, we find that we are done with distractions. We are done searching for love. We don't look for a love fulfillment in the latest book or the latest trend in the church or the latest man or woman. When we stop the struggle to find love, and focus on the journey of soul surrender, then we become more about surrendering to God and less about serving ourselves. As strange as it seems, coming to the end of self is a good thing. At the end of self, we discover this truth: God is love. At first it may feel quite uncomfortable, coming to the end of self, because here we do not control our souls' longing to be filled. When our soul surrenders, we allow God to do what he does best: love us.

This is what we were created for. If we can stop seeking our own fulfillment long enough, we will realize that all other sources of love do not ultimately satisfy the longings of our souls. There may be a moment of satisfaction, a false sense of love, but it doesn't truly minister to the depths of the soul. Only God can do that. When we receive God's love, we no longer want people or things to fill us. We want to relax; to stretch out in God's presence. We are safe. We can allow our souls' longings to be fully exposed and to be loved completely. When the soul surrenders, the authentic love of God is realized.

We can all share a time when we sought out love: a time when we tried to fulfill our love longings with someone or something, only to be disappointed. Some of us carry heavy burdens because of love (or what we thought was love) that has been lost. These burdens weigh us down. We feel as if we are carrying a backpack full of rocks through life. We are tired. We are burdened and burned out.

However, the end of self is a new day. The God of love says, "Come to me, all you who are weary and burdened, and I will give you rest. Take my yoke upon you and learn from me, for I am gentle and humble in heart, and you will find rest for your souls. For my yoke is easy and my burden is light" (Matt. 11:28–30). We can choose (God always gives us the choice) to come to him. If we choose to surrender our love longings for his filling, then truly we will find the answer to our question, "Am I loved?"

GOING FURTHER IN SURRENDER
Chapter One

1. What is your all-time favorite childhood memory?

2. Think about a time as a child when you asked, "Do you love me, Daddy?" How was your question answered?

3. From the reading in the first chapter of *When the Soul Surrenders*, what are your thoughts and/or feelings about this statement: "We were not created to search for love, we were created to receive God's love."

4. Read the creation story beginning in Genesis Chapters 1 and 2. Think about all that God created. What aspect of God's creation do you enjoy most? Why?

5. Look at the following scriptures. What are the benefits you receive by believing God is love?

> 1 John 4:16b
>
> Psalm 62:1, 5
>
> Psalm 86:4
>
> Isaiah 55:3
>
> Matthew 11:28–30
>
> John 3:16
>
> Ephesians 2:4–5

6. Take a moment now, be still and let God love you.

CHAPTER TWO

Thou Art With Me

When the lonely soul surrenders,
belonging is established.

> "But you are a chosen people, a royal
> priesthood, a holy nation, a people belonging
> to God, that you may declare the praises of
> him who called you out of darkness into his
> wonderful light."
>
> (1 Peter 2:9)

Looming in the depth of many souls is this question: "Am I
alone?" It is in this questioning that the human longing to
belong to someone or something is brought forth to our
awareness. If we stop to ponder this disquieting question, we
may be tempted to succumb to fear. When our lonesome soul is
reminded of an unfulfilled longing, we come face-to-face with
the tormenting fear of being forsaken forever. It may seem
strange, then, to suggest that the truth is, we *do* belong, even if
we *feel* alone.

Andy revealed to me that she often felt very alone. She says that learning to be alone was the safer course of action.

> I like to be alone. It is safe. The anger in my childhood home seemed to penetrate every fiber of my being. It is as if I have taken every pain, every fight, and every smashed glass and carried them with me like a shield of protection. I put up walls to keep people away. My walls consist of anger, bitterness, fear, and an inability to trust. I am often mad at something or someone. Always, the safer course of action for me is to be alone.
>
> When I was three or maybe four years old, my babysitter took me to her church. I can remember sitting on the floor with my skinny little legs tightly crossed, listening intently. I was like a baby sparrow craning its neck to receive nourishment from its mother. I heard about Jesus. I didn't know who he was or where he was. Then we sang songs about Jesus. One song we sang told me "Jesus loves the little children, all the children of the world; red, yellow, black or white, they are precious in his sight." Then we sang another song: "Jesus loves me, this I know, for the Bible tells me so." I thought to myself, "If Jesus loves all the little children, if Jesus loves me and the Bible says it is so, then I will love him back."
>
> I liked going to Sunday school. I don't know how many times I went there, but I always felt I belonged. It was a bright warm light in my dark, cold world. I felt safe. The teacher smelled like gardenias. She smiled at me and gently touched my cheek. All the people knew my name. I got lots of hugs and smiles. People were happy. For the first time, I can remember feeling special, as if I belonged to something good and very

important. Some time later, we moved away from that little church. My connection was cut off. I was alone.

Andy remembers a frightening time when she was left alone.

I walked home from school. When I reached the house, I found a note pinned to the front door that read: "We moved. Be back soon to get you." I had to go to the bathroom, but the door was locked. I sat and waited, and wondered why I didn't know we were moving.

Andy told me she waited a very long time until someone came to pick her up and take her to the new place.

At the core of every soul is a longing to belong, to be a part of something bigger. To feel included in the plan. No wonder so many of us are not willing to consider surrendering our all to God; frankly, we just don't believe that we are part of his plan.

We simply do not trust his plan. We doubt that we really do belong to him. And we wonder if our lives are really connected to someone bigger than us. We fear that if we lie bare before the King of the Universe, or if we fall face down at the foot of the cross, we will find ... nothing.

There is no convincing anyone that God is ever-present. If I say to someone who feels isolated, cut off, and alone, "God is with you," I might just as well give him or her a slap in the face. So many times I have heard these sentiments: "So sorry to hear your husband passed on. God is with you." "What a shame your boyfriend broke up with you. Oh well, God is with you." Or perhaps, "It must be difficult to be fired from your job, but remember, God is with you." How trite these words sound. How often I have used them myself. It is like using a fluffy cotton ball to try to stop a gaping wound from bleeding.

Aloneness is painful. Facing the depth of our aloneness, which is another aspect of the discipline of surrender, is how we know that we do belong to God. God's presence is experienced and integrated within the depth of the soul when we embrace our own personal Gethsemane—that gut-wrenching place where we are completely alone. That place that Jesus experienced dying on the cross. It is then that we will die to self and live for him, believing (and not because some well-meaning person said so) that God is truly with us.

We cling so tightly to possessions and people, hoping to create a sense of belonging. I once shared with a friend that we will ultimately have to give up everything and everyone except for Jesus. We can hold on to him forever. She responded by insisting that was a very depressing thought. But we must admit that it is true. Think about it: we will ultimately have to give up everything and everyone except for Jesus.

Not only can we hold on to Jesus forever, he wants us to learn how to do it now. He wants to teach us the value of belonging intimately to him. He declares that we are his and he wants to be with us.

Here is the crux of the matter: How will we experience God's presence if we are not willing to consider our aloneness? If we never allow our souls to delve into the crevice of aloneness, how will we know that God is present?

Remember the story of Moses? He was a man in the Bible who experienced a privileged childhood. But he discovered the importance of the complete abandonment of his possessions and of his Egyptian people, so that he might experience belonging to God. Moses wanted to belong to God. He believed that living in the presence of God was the only way to give himself and the people of God, the Israelites, an authentic identity, a sense of belonging, a hope, and a future.

Moses said to God:

> If your Presence does not go with us, do not send
> us up from here. How will anyone know that you

are pleased with me and with your people unless you go with us? What else will distinguish me and your people from all the other people on the face of the earth? (Exod. 33:15–16)

God had already told Moses that he would be with him: "My Presence will go with you, and I will give you rest" (Exod. 33:14).

Moses learned the value of abandonment of self for belonging to God. There is a modern-day story of a child that also illustrates this important principal of God's presence in our place of abandonment.

Do you remember the story of Baby Jessica, who fell into a well more than twenty years ago in Midland, Texas? She was trapped twenty-two feet underground for 58 hours. During her ordeal, paramedics lowered a television microphone to hear her, and at one point they heard her singing songs like "Jesus Loves Me" that she had learned in Sunday school. Like the oxygen and heat that were sent into the well, little Jessica comforted herself with songs proclaiming the presence of Jesus. "Little ones to him belong."

Robert O'Donnell, one of the paramedics who pulled Jessica out of the well, stayed with her throughout the rescue mission. He was cited as the one who was there the longest, trying to save Baby Jessica. I wonder if it was human presence or the comfort of Jesus that sustained this child as she lay prone in the depths of a well, with one leg up, and one leg down (Casey 2002).

Like the story of Baby Jessica falling into a deep well, a good friend of mine slipped into a deep, dark depression. Nothing could reach her. She was isolated and locked up in her home for days. She could barely function. She was emotionally desolate. She felt cut off from God, and felt safe with no one.

I knocked on her front door. No answer. I quietly went in, and I found her lying on the living room sofa. I told her, "I am here to sit with you, to be with you in your pain. I won't talk to you or bother you, I will sit here, next to you, all day or until you tell me to leave. I will silently pray." I wanted to offer her my presence as if I could somehow be a vessel of the Holy Spirit, breathing life into her deserted soul. I wanted her to know Jesus was sitting right beside her. I wanted her to know that she was not alone; that she belongs to him.

When we seize the opportunity to minister in this way to fellow sojourners, we have the glorious occasion to be in the precious company of Jesus. I learned I could be still and quiet and pray, finding connection and a sense of belonging to God. I filled up with the power of the Holy Spirit, which then over-flowed, carrying the hope of belonging to my abandoned friend. The presence of God was with us, pumping strength into me to pray for her, while at the same time renewing her spirit.

God has created us with a longing to belong to him and to one another. When we experience the power of his presence through the Holy Spirit, there is connection.

A longing for belonging is beautifully illustrated by Our Lord himself in the Gospel of Matthew:

> Then Jesus went with his disciples to a place called
> Gethsemane, and he said to them, "Sit here while
> I go over there and pray." He took Peter and the
> two sons of Zebedee along with him, and he began
> to be sorrowful and troubled. Then he said to
> them, "My soul is overwhelmed with sorrow to the
> point of death. Stay here and keep watch with me"
> (Matt. 26:36–38).

"Stay here and keep watch with me," Jesus said. He wanted to know that his companions were not only with him in prayer, but also in proximity. His soul was overwhelmed with sorrow. He couldn't possibly face the pain before him without the closeness of human companions.

> Going a little farther, he fell with his face to the ground and prayed, "My Father, if it is possible, may this cup be taken from me. Yet not as I will, but as you will." Then he returned to his disciples and found them sleeping. "Could you men not keep watch with me for one hour?" he asked Peter (Matt. 26:39–40).

Jesus longed to know that his closest friends were with him in his greatest time of need. Yet he was forsaken, alone. He prepared to face his own death. The assurance that God the Father was with him in his greatest hour of need had to be enough. He wrestled with his Father's plan, but finally came to terms with God's will for his life: "My Father, if it is not possible for this cup to be taken away unless I drink it, may your will be done" (Matt. 26:42). Jesus then embraced Gethsemane. He agonized in choosing God's will above his own. He knew that on the cross he would be forsaken; he felt the weight of his choice in the cross. His burden would give all people a chance to belong. We are reminded of this truth in the Bible, which says: "...he humbled himself and became obedient to death—even death on a cross!" (Phil. 2:8b).

Jesus hung on the cross alone. All who said they would follow him abandoned him. As he took the sins of the world on himself, even God, his Father, looked away. Jesus faced the ultimate fear we all have that makes us wonder if we will be forsaken forever. But he made sure that all who would believe in him would always belong. He said, "Never will I leave you; never will I forsake you" (Heb. 13:5).

Do you believe this? Do you believe in the power of God's presence when it is just you and God? When you are completely alone in your greatest time of need, do you believe that God himself is with you? "Never will I leave you; never will I forsake you." That is his word, his promise. Jesus Christ says he will never leave me. I write it and together we read it, but do we know it in the depths of our lonesome souls?

There is nothing else I need for this day except to embrace this truth: Jesus will never leave me or forsake me.

As I read these words, something begins to happen. I begin to cry. I can't help but wonder if the soul wounds of the people around me would find healing if they whole-heartedly believed that they are not alone.

His words, "Never will I leave you; never will I forsake you," do not remove us from our state of aloneness, but simply and beautifully blanket us with a sense of warmth, as if someone has come and laid a warm comforter over our trembling bodies. As we trust in his presence, we find warmth and oxygen for our abandoned souls. For just a moment, in this surrendered place we are able to sense his glorious presence. In our longing for belonging, if we humble ourselves and embrace our moments of abandonment, we will find a friend standing there and, maybe for the first time, we will recognize his presence.

I can't say that it feels good to embrace our aloneness in the discipline of surrender. But I am learning, as I hope you will, to trust that there is a glorious value to be understood here. When we face our fear of aloneness in the presence of God, we find belonging in the depths of our souls. In my meek understanding of absolute abandonment to God and to his will, I can, and I will, choose to trust his word. And his word says that he will never leave me or forsake me. Imagine that. Little ones and big ones—we do belong to him.

Abandoned

Utterly abandoned to the Holy Ghost!
Seeking all His fullness, whatever the cost;
Cutting all the moorings, launching in the deep
Of His mighty power—strong to save and keep.

Utterly abandoned to the Holy Ghost!
Oh! The sinking, sinking, until self is lost!
Until the emptied vessel lies broken at His feet;
Waiting till His filling shall make the work complete.

Utterly abandoned to the will of God;
Seeking for no other path than my Master trod;
Leaving ease and pleasure, making Him my choice,
Waiting for His guidance, listening for His voice.

Utterly abandoned! No will of my own;
For time and for eternity, His, and His alone;
All my plans and purposes lost in His sweet will,
Having nothing, yet in Him all things possessing still.

Utterly abandoned! It's so sweet to be
Captive in His bonds of love, yet wondrously free;
Free from sin's entanglements, free from doubt and fear,
Free from every worry, burden, grief, or care.

Utterly abandoned! Oh, the rest is sweet,
As I tarry, waiting, at His blessed feet;
Waiting for the coming of the Guest divine,
Who my inmost being will perfectly refine.

Lo! He comes and fills me, Holy Spirit sweet!
I, in Him, am satisfied! I, in Him, complete!
And the light within my soul will nevermore grow dim
While I keep my covenant—abandoned unto Him!

Author unknown

GOING FURTHER IN SURRENDER
Chapter Two

1. What special occasions have you been invited to attend or participate in?

2. What does this statement mean to you? "At the core of every soul is a longing to belong, to be a part of something bigger; to feel included in the plan."

3. God tells Moses that his presence will go with him (Exod. 33:14). Why would this be so important to Moses?

4. Can you recall a time when you felt God's presence strongly?

5. When have you been tempted to doubt the scripture, "Never will I leave you; never will I forsake you?"

6. Read Psalm 23. Read Psalm 23 again, slowly. Breathe in each word and personalize it. What is God saying to you today through this Psalm?

7. Take some time now to reflect on your life. Remember the people that God has provided to keep watch with you. Make a list of those people and thank God for his goodness in providing people to be with you heart and soul.

8. How does knowing you belong to God affect your ability to surrender your all to him?

9. What do you need to surrender today?

CHAPTER THREE

Poor in Spirit

*When the humble soul surrenders,
riches are realized.*

"The jewel of joy is given to the impoverished
spirit, not the affluent. God's delight is
received upon surrender, not awarded upon
conquest. The first step to joy is a plea
for help; an acknowledgment of moral
destitution ... God's delight is born in
the parched soil of destitution rather than
the fertile ground of achievement."

Max Lucado (1999)

I could barely hear her words. Andy whispered:

My Aunt Nelly died. She committed suicide. She was
beaten so badly by her fifth husband, she was beyond
recognition.

When I was a young girl, I spent the summer months with her and her two girls, my older cousins. I liked being with my cousins and my aunt. I felt like the spoiled baby sister. My aunt lived in Blythe, California, a barren desert area that some would think of as a wasteland, but I found the Colorado River to be a precious jewel. The river became a refreshing treasure in my life. I loved the days we spent on the riverbanks, swimming in the brisk water and floating on old black, lopsided, rubber inner tubes. At night we often walked to town to indulge in an ice cream parfait.

One summer, Aunt Nelly sewed me an outfit to match my older cousins'. I wore the crisp cotton ensemble like a famous Hollywood star. I can still see the smile on my aunt's face as I pranced around the room and she announced: "Here she comes, Miss America."

She had been missing for a few days. Finally, she was found in a cheap motel room in downtown Culver City. My dad tried to find her husband to tell him the bad news. It took a few more days, but finally he was found in a local bar. He was taken to identify my aunt's body. I guess he felt ashamed about what he had done to her. You know, he beat her up pretty bad—so bad that he refused to allow the girls (my aunt's daughters) to see their lifeless mother. She was cremated.

Our family was sitting around in the small Culver City apartment. Every time the phone would ring, my cousin would jump up and pronounce with great zeal, "that's got to be Mom calling, I'll get it." I was so excited. I thought, "maybe she isn't dead. I'll find her. I'll find my Aunt Nelly!"

People express grief in many different ways. In the above story, the overall approach to the death of Aunt Nelly was denial.

Andy went on to explain more about that time in her life.

> My mom was the one who told me Aunt Nelly was
> dead. I started to cry. Before I could feel the depth of
> my sorrow, my mom handed me a Valium and a glass
> of water. At the memorial service, I wore a bright
> orange outfit. My cousins dressed me. They said I
> needed to be cheerful and joyful, because it would
> please their mother. I felt stupid. I was embarrassed.
> Everyone was dressed in muted colors, and there I
> was, like a clown at a kid's birthday party. Nothing
> about my outside appearance represented the inside.
> I felt confused, angry, mad, and sad, and no one was
> able to help me understand my feelings.
>   For years to follow, I would see women who
> resembled my deceased aunt in the market or at a
> restaurant. I would cry and think, "that's her, I just
> know it!" My aching spirit longed to see her just one
> more time. I did not accept her death. Somehow,
> I thought, I would find her. I would fix this tragedy.
> I would make it right.

Grief plays an important role in soul surrender. Grief invites us to experience a depth of ourselves and a depth of Jesus that cannot be manufactured in any other manner. If we are encouraged to grieve properly, we will find we can live properly. To grieve well is to live well.

I see the idea of grief presented in chapter five of the Gospel of Matthew. It is in the section called the Beatitudes. Beatitude is a Latin word that means "supreme blessedness." The first beatitude that Jesus speaks about is being poor in spirit. Jesus says that those who possess an attitude of poverty of spirit are supremely blessed. One commentary I read suggested that a better word for "blessed" would be "fortunate." Fortunate "are the poor in spirit, for theirs is the kingdom of heaven" (Matt. 5:3).

Being poor in spirit is a difficult mind-set to grasp. No one really wants to be poor in any way. But it is people who are poor in spirit who have an accurate view of themselves in relationship to God. Author Louis Evely, in his 1964 book *That Man Is You,* says it this way:

> Fortunate are those who are willing to let themselves be censured by the word of God, to re-examine their views, to believe they haven't yet understood a thing, to be taken by surprise, to have their minds changed, to see their convictions, their principles, their tidy systems and everything they took for granted swept out from under them, and to face the fact, once and for all, that there's no such thing as a matter of course and that God can ask anything.

If it is true that the impoverished spirit is fortunate, and that "blessed are the poor in spirit, for theirs is the kingdom of heaven," what exactly is the point for us, in relationship to soul surrender? In the discipline of surrender, we are asked to foster an attitude of acceptance of the demands of God's Kingdom. God asks each of us to be alive in Christ and to die to self.

Have you ever wondered what it means to die to self? Who even wants to think about such a thing? I have tried in my flesh (our self-indulgent nature) to die to self. I have attempted to control the workings of the Holy Spirit through emotional distress, using such methods as depression, withdrawal, isolation, and even focusing on suicidal thoughts. This is merely the flesh desiring death and the mind taking control of the self-dying process. Of course, there are other more acceptable fleshly ways of dying to self, such as creating for oneself a lifestyle of crisis or chaos, or spending one's time on distractions. We make meals for the sick, we lead Bible studies, and we clean the church kitchen.

Although these are admirable acts of service, they may only be substitutes for true dying to self. They don't teach us to be poor in spirit—they usually just make us tired.

We fear the real thing. We dread it. We long to cling to all sides of our old ways of dying to self. Dying to self is not something we do; it is something we accept. Dying to self is a letting go of trying to substantiate the self. If I could say it simply, it would be this: Get over yourself! There is no ten-step program to die to self. That would be doing, not being, and poor in spirit is something you are, not something you do. It is an attitude, not an accomplishment.

We are to be with Jesus in whatever place he has us. Notice when Andy's aunt committed suicide, no one was "allowed" to be in pain. The family handled this tragic situation by using the mechanism of denial. I am not faulting them. I am only suggesting that if Andy could have expressed her grief openly, and shown her true emotions, then she would have had the opportunity to experience the authenticity of being poor in spirit. That, in turn, would have allowed her to develop a foundation for healthy grieving.

Imagine if the young Andy had been allowed to weep and mourn. What if her parents simply said, "It's OK to be sad. We are sad too." Instead, her pain, her poverty, was masked with Valium. It was as if she were told it's not OK to feel. We must numb the pain. Let us pretend there is no poverty here. Yet it is in the grieving times of life that we begin to embrace poverty of spirit. It is at these times that we most often find we must humbly trust God by becoming empty before him.

Another aspect of the beatitude poor in spirit is that we cannot empty ourselves. We must wait on God, for it is through the workings of the Holy Spirit that this work is accomplished. Our job is to be a willing vessel. We are to see opportunities to be poor in spirit as things to be seized, not things to be avoided or fixed.

He empties and he fills. I am aware of my own desire to have him fill me quickly. We are often drawn to a prayer of filling and glorifying and guiding and showing and doing. People who are poor in spirit understand the value of waiting on God. People who are poor in spirit have learned to be quiet in the emptiness of their souls. They know there is a war going on that has been waged between the flesh and the soul, but they have learned to trust in God, who will always prevail. And when he does, it will be a glorious filling, not a man-made work of the flesh, but the glorious work of God. Why would we settle for anything else?

We often handle painful emotions by using substances such as alcohol, drugs, caffeine, or sugar. We settle for the quick fix; seeking a happier self through food, sex, pornography, shopping, and religious activities. We are drawn to anything that will help us avoid pain in the poor-in-spirit times of our lives.

There is an easy way to test your own growth in this area by completing the following statement: I want _____.

What was your first response? Just recently, I found myself in a "wanting" place. I decided that we needed new bedroom furniture. I was looking at television ads promising no interest or payments for one year. I was reading the advertisements in the newspaper trying to figure out how we might buy some new furniture. I found myself saying over and over, "I want this bedroom set." With my thoughts focused on this, I began to think about how I could buy it on credit. As I am writing about this recent experience, I am struck with the realization that when my mind is filled with "I want," I must immediately be still and wait.

Jesus reminded me that, "Foxes have holes and birds of the air have nests, but the Son of Man has no place to lay his head" (Matt. 8:20).

Do we ever say, "I *want* to know Christ?" The Apostle Paul said, "I want to know Christ and the power of his resurrection and the fellowship of sharing in his sufferings, becoming like him in his death, . . ." (Phil. 3:10). I believe everyone would agree that we want to share in the power of his resurrection, but do we ever say, "I want to share in the fellowship of Christ's sufferings?" Or, "I want to become like Jesus in his death?"

"I want to know Christ and the power of his resurrection and the fellowship of sharing in his sufferings, becoming like him in his death." Are these your desires?

I was filled to the brim with anger as my pastor husband was packing for a three-day weekend retreat with the elders of our church. I felt as if he wanted to get away from me. I can't say I blame him, as I often long to get away from myself. He had about twenty minutes before he had to leave. In fear and trembling, he asked, "Andrea, what's wrong?" We began to argue. We stopped listening to one another. No one was waiting or hearing, we just wanted desperately to express our own flesh to one another. I sat on the floor. I looked at him and said, "I'm spiritually empty and I don't feel as if we are doing anything as a couple to help that." Finally, quiet. The arguing stopped. There was only a realization and acceptance of truth. I wasn't blaming my husband for my spiritual emptiness, I was simply confessing it. He asked me what he could do to help me. He wanted to help. He wanted me to be OK, to be fixed. (I am sure he also wanted to have this "mess" all tidy before he left for the elders' retreat.)

Coming to the end of one's self is not a tidy work. It is a messy outpouring of truth, a spilling over of confession, and a gut-wrenching repentance. Blaming is over. Expectations have ceased. I expressed to my husband that I was empty. I so wanted to blame him for my feelings of emptiness. I longed to have more spiritual connection with him, but I did not want any man-made answers. I wanted the Holy Spirit to guide me. I asked him to pray about this while he was away. He agreed to do so.

Have you come to the end of yourself? Good. There is a filling that can only come from the hand of Jesus Christ when he reaches down by the power of his Spirit and fills us up. But we must be empty of self. He can't fill up someone who is already full. And when we find ourselves empty and needing his filling, we must fight the urge to fix the problem by expecting or demanding that others fill us. We must be willing to stay in the poor-in-spirit state until the Lord, through the Holy Spirit, fills us.

David expresses this idea beautifully in Psalm 51:16–17. "You do not delight in sacrifice, or I would bring it; you do not take pleasure in burnt offerings. The sacrifices of God are a broken spirit; a broken and contrite heart."

A person who understands that a broken spirit and a broken and contrite heart are a delight to God is a person who understands the benefits of being poor in spirit. The poor in spirit are humble, beautiful people. They have found the treasure of their own poverty; they are able to touch the kingdom of heaven. People who are poor in spirit have an accurate view of themselves in relationship to God. They have accepted that they are morally and spiritually bankrupt and unable to survive on their own strength. They know that the only Benevolent Helper is God.

In modern times, we are inundated with the religious idea of a name-it-and-claim-it prosperity gospel. We have come dangerously close to losing the most beautiful aspect of the Christian faith. That is, we have divorced ourselves from the benefits of a broken spirit, a broken and contrite heart. Somehow, we believe, and are often taught, that we are to bypass this part of Christianity. We avoid the verses such as "For to me, to live is Christ and to die is gain" (Phil. 1:21). We ignore the wisdom of our forefathers like the Apostle Paul. He found a depth of contentment through his own poverty of spirit; that is, sharing in Christ's suffering.

If we seek to bypass the suffering, the poor-in-spirit times on our journey, then we miss out on knowing the whole of the one we claim to serve.

As I was writing this chapter, I was faced with the opportunity to experience this poor-in-spirit place. An older man in our congregation had offended me by publicly speaking to me in sexual undertones. I confronted him. Later, my husband and another elder confronted him. He was broken over his blunder. He wanted to apologize to me in person. I felt sick every time I thought of seeing him. Yet, the Spirit of God was gently prodding me through my writing. I knew I had to face this man.

I felt shame and brokenness over this man's insensitivity toward me. I felt sad, and I felt deep sorrow for the offense. Not his, but mine. I am no better than this man. I have spoken hurtful words. I have used sexual undertones. Who am I to think that he even owes me an apology? But, I knew that part of his and my own healing process would be to face this man with as much grace as possible. Therefore, I needed to face him with a poor-in-spirit attitude. As he shared his heart, and asked for forgiveness, I was able to humbly accept it, and reach out and touch his hand and say, "I forgive you; you are my brother in Christ." This experience allowed me, in a small way, to embrace the poor-in-spirit attitude through what I like to call "taking the lower position," the humble position with this brother-in-Christ.

The Kingdom of Heaven is found within the soul when we experience the deepest feelings of the lower position. We must learn not to fear destitution, but to embrace it. It must break God's heart every time he sees us desperately, yet feebly, trying to fix or cover over our experiences of poverty of spirit. As we allow our own impoverished spirit to freely surface, it will feel as if we are waiting for a drink of water in a parched desert. We wait and receive the grace of God spilling forward as we are drenched with an inexpressible and glorious joy. When we are willing to embrace poverty of spirit, a precious jewel has been found, a treasure meant just for us. Grab it! Hold it closely. And never let it go. When the soul surrenders, it treasures the poor-in-spirit times of life.

GOING FURTHER IN SURRENDER
Chapter Three

1. Think of a time in your life when you felt especially blessed (fortunate).

2. What are your thoughts/feelings about this idea: "God's delight is received upon surrender, not awarded upon conquest."

3. Whom do you consider to be a humble person? What qualities about this person do you admire?

4. When you are spiritually empty, in what ways are you tempted to fill yourself?

5. Read and write out the following scriptures:

   Matthew 8:20

   Philippians 3:10

   Psalm 51:16–17

6. According to God's word, what are some of the benefits of being poor in spirit?

7. Is God asking you to embrace poverty of spirit by taking the lower position with someone in your life? If so, how and when will you do this?

CHAPTER FOUR

A Guided Tour

When the wayward soul surrenders,
guidance is given.

"Whether you turn to the right or to the left,
your ears will hear a voice behind you, saying,
'This is the way; walk in it.'"

(Isa. 30:21)

Andy's eyes lit up as she explained a point of surrender:

I felt like a volcano had erupted and spewed forth vile,
black emotions from some deep place within my soul;
an outpouring of gushing sobs; screams directed at
God, with questions: "Where were you, God?" and "Are
you really good?" I could not move. I needed to know
where he was when I was a little girl.

Like a child throwing a tantrum, I demanded that
he speak to me. I begged him to explain why he left
me in the hands of abuse, violence, neglect, and
unresolved grief? I couldn't stop crying. I kept yelling
out to God, demanding his presence to speak to me.

I asked him, "Lord, how can I claim you as my Lord and Savior of my life if I don't trust you with my past? How can I proclaim you as a good guide if I have doubts about your goodness?"

I could feel him taking the hand of my soul. I felt as if he were leading me through a maze, like a maze of mirrors at a carnival. The maze was my life, and his voice gently guided me. Turn to the right, my child; now turn to the left.

We stopped at a mirror and looked in at a particular point of my life. I saw my babysitter, who took me with her to church. I saw her parents, who welcomed me into their warm, loving home. I thought it was so cute how they covered their toaster with a quilted cozy. I could smell the aroma of chocolate chip cookies baking.

I saw my oak tree on Sylvia Street. God explained that he had created that giant oak tree for my joy, comfort, and sense of belonging to something bigger than me.

He showed me my best friend and her mother, who had offered me a home away from home all through elementary school. He told me that they were his provision for my developmental years. And then there was Mr. Levy, my favorite fourth grade teacher. Apparently, he was God's gift to me.

I saw Aunt Nelly sitting at her sewing machine, humming the song "Crazy" by Patsy Cline, while smiling at me. And then I saw Granny Elsie baking an apple pie from scratch. He told me that they were my inspiration for sewing and baking. I could not stop the flood of tears. At that moment, I understood that God cared about the little things important to me like sewing and baking. I thought, "He is a good guide."

I cried for joy as I embraced the reality that he indeed was, and is, a trustworthy guide.

I discovered that many of my childhood longings were cared for by God's goodness. He gave me guideposts and mentors along the way to lovingly lead me. He assured me that, although I felt adrift in this world, he was guiding me.

He was with me. I believe that now. He watched over me carefully. I could trust in his guidance for my past, my present and my future. I knew in my heart, soul, and mind that he is a good guide.

For the first time in her life, Andy boldly questioned her childhood and the character of God. She asked, "Are you good?" At last she was able to take all her years of pain, problems and confusion about God's goodness and reach out with a firm grip on the truth that God is, and always has been, a trustworthy guide. Trusting in the providence of God would be the cornerstone of her emotional healing and of her ability to surrender to him. This was a very important turning point in her life.

Her revelation reminded me of the story of Joseph in the Bible. Joseph is given the opportunity to confront his abusive brothers. He expresses his own revelation of truth about God's goodness in leading him when he says, "You intended to harm me, but God intended it for good" (Gen. 50:20).

As I prepared to write this chapter, I had to fight the urge to bypass it or sugarcoat it. It seemed a lofty task to write about a good God who tenderly leads his people when so often his people face terrible trials. I didn't believe I could communicate God's sovereign guidance without sounding trite. I certainly don't want to appear insensitive to anyone's past or present trial. As I wrestled with my own insecurities before the Lord, I heard him gently say, "This is the way; walk in it" (Isa. 30:21).

So, I am taking the next step and suggesting that perhaps our struggle in surrender does not come from what was lacking in our childhoods, or what we experienced in awkward adolescence, or even the adversities of adulthood, but instead from our belief about God's guidance in our lives. At some point, we have to stop and boldly ask: "Do I believe God was present? Do I believe God is present now? Do I believe he is good, always?" Our ability to trust in his good guidance prompts surrender. Conversely, our lack of trust impairs our willingness to surrender.

I imagine Elisabeth Elliot wondered about God's good guidance as she struggled to understand the murder of her missionary husband. By God's grace, she concluded, "Either we are adrift in chaos or we are individuals, created, loved, upheld, and placed purposefully, exactly where we are. Can you believe that? Can you trust God for that?" (Elliot 2004).

He wants us to believe in him as our good guide for all of life. We must look to him for truth and not trust in our circumstances, our spouse, our children, our jobs, our pleasures or our pains. He is the living, guiding Sovereign of the entire universe, and he promises, "I will never leave you nor forsake you" (Josh. 1:5). So then why is it difficult for us to embrace his omniscient direction in our lives, especially when tough things are happening?

Sure it's easy to trust that God is good when good things are happening. The day I won a trip to Maui, I was overjoyed with God's goodness. When I heard my name called out on the radio station, I started crying like a baby and praising God for his goodness. I even thanked him for guiding me in that moment to listen to the radio. I thought, "Because of his guidance, I actually won."

When God is guiding us with good gifts, like vacations, we are all willing to proclaim his goodness, submit to his guidance, praise him and give him the glory. But how do we respond to God's guidance in our lives when something bad happens?

I heard a heartbreaking story that made me wonder about God's goodness in one family's life. Apparently they were traveling with their younger children to visit their oldest son, who was away at college. A bracket from a truck fell and punctured their minivan's gas tank. The resulting fire and explosion killed Peter, six weeks old; Elizabeth, three years old; Hank, seven; Sam, nine; Joe, eleven; and Ben, thirteen.

It is difficult to view God as a good guide during a tragedy such as this. Yet, the father was thankful they died quickly. He said that he understood that trials come and that faith will be tested. If it is not tested, then it is empty.

I can't imagine facing the loss of a child. Dr. C. Everett Koop lost his son. He says this about God's guidance: "If God is all-powerful, then naturally everything that happens—everything—falls under his complete control at all times" (Yancy 2001).

There are times when horrific things happen. They seem to be beyond comprehension. They are so bad and so ugly that no one wants to look. They are unspeakable. The Holocaust comes to mind.

I recently watched a documentary in which Holocaust survivors were interviewed. They each talked about some of the atrocities they had experienced. Just hearing the stories made me flinch and want to look away. The survivors interviewed had become Christians (www.jewsforjesus.org). Somehow they were able to reconcile their history with this truth: God *is* a good guide.

This is more than "choosing to believe" or engaging in a "just do it" kind of mental exercise. It is more than having a positive attitude. It is difficult to explain, but perhaps those who come the closest to experiencing hell on earth are the ones who are most able to come the closest to the Holy One. They are able, through tremendous brokenness, humility, and survival, to embrace God's goodness. This unshakable reality does not erase the memories, but profoundly becomes the anchor that holds them steady, and enables them to proclaim God is a good guide. We can trust in his guidance in and through our lives.

Life is full of blessings, and life is full of trials. I wonder how people get through difficult life trials if they don't believe God is a good guide. My dear sojourner, isn't it time to choose to surrender your wayward soul to his sovereign guidance? Your unwavering trust in his good guidance will make the difference between living out your life full of bitterness or full of blessings.

In our humanity, we struggle to believe that our God is a good guide. We question him and wonder about his plan for "our" lives. After all, each of us surmises, it is *my* life. Let's look at a group of God's children who fluctuate between bitterness and blessing. They are known as the Israelites.

God's children were in slavery for many years. With the help of God, Moses led them from slavery to freedom. It is remarkable to read about how God guided them. "By day the Lord went ahead of them in a pillar of cloud to guide them on their way and by night in a pillar of fire to give them light, so that they could travel by day or night" (Exod. 13:21).

Imagine thousands of people who had been in slavery for 430 years being lead out by God himself in the form of a billowing cloud and a glowing fire! However, as time marched on, the pilgrimage became too long, too difficult. The miracle of the daily provision of manna became distasteful. The people began to grumble, and to blame Moses for their plight. God's children no longer felt blessed, but bitter. They were no longer proclaiming God as a good guide, saying, "Wow is God"; instead, they were saying "Woe is me." They were so perplexed by God's guidance, they mournfully exclaimed, "If only we had died by the Lord's hand in Egypt! There we sat around pots of meat and ate all the food we wanted, but you have brought us out into this desert to starve this entire assembly to death" (Exod. 16:3).

The desolate Israelites remembered Egypt through rose-tinted glasses. They dreamed of their time in slavery like it was a long-lost lover. They couldn't see God's love leading them. They were wearing blinders of fear and discomfort that caused them to view their deliverance as worse than slavery.

When our deliverer leads us out of a bad situation, he may lead us into a place that appears or feels worse. During these times, our faith is tested and refined, and we don't like it. In these seemingly worse situations, our natural tendency is to doubt God's good guidance.

At first, we may be excited about a new adventure. When we get married, or have our first child, we are thrilled. When we finally get to the mission field, or land our very first real job out of college, we are thankful for God's good guidance in our lives. But all too often, when the honeymoon is over, or the baby has colic, or the mission field is too hot, or the job is wearing, we waver in our trust in God's guidance. Like the Israelites, we begin to doubt God's sovereign guidance in our lives. We wonder if God brought us to this place to die. Then we must remember: surrender is always a type of dying to self.

During life's trials, we have the wonderful opportunity to embrace and trust in God's leadership. We may feel as if we are being led in circles in the penetrating heat of the desert. Life can become so uncomfortable that we want to give up on God and return to whatever we knew before the journey began, even if it's slavery.

God is leading. He is a good guide. God led the Israelites out of a bad situation in Egypt, through what felt like a worse situation in the desert, and finally, after 40 years, he brought them into the Promised Land. He wants us to develop an unflinching trust that he is leading us. God is asking each of us to have courage and follow him. He says, "This is the way; walk in it" (Isa. 30:21).

It is in the hot, barren desert of your surrendered soul that God will often do his best work, if you surrender your way for his. Only in the desert will you see the beauty of a lone cactus flower. Only in the desert will you view the twisted Joshua tree. Only in the desert will we look up and encounter the universe of stars. Then we realize the world does not revolve around us.

Think of that desert as the valley mentioned in Psalm 23: "Yea, though I walk through the valley of the shadow of death" (Psalm 23:4, King James Version). It does not say I die there, or stop there—but rather that I *walk through.*

Here is a promise that God will not leave you in the difficult place forever. He is walking you through. Surrender. Walk with him. He is showing you the way, while at the same time teaching you that his guidance is trustworthy. When the soul surrenders to God's direction, bitterness is replaced with blessing. Just as God revealed his guidance to Andy:

> He was with me. I believe that now. He watched over me carefully. I could trust in his guidance for my past, my present and my future.

When your wayward soul surrenders, he will reveal his goodness to you. You can trust in his guidance.

GOING FURTHER IN SURRENDER
Chapter Four

1. Can you think of a time in your past when God was guiding you and you didn't know it at the time, but can clearly see it now?

2. Why would trusting in the providence of a good God be the cornerstone of emotional healing and the ability to surrender (or not) to him?

3. What current trial(s) in your life make you doubt that God is good and that he is in control of the past, present and future? Or, if you are not currently facing a personal trial, then what current event makes you question God's good guidance?

4. Read these verses about God's good guidance. What does your soul need from God's word today? When a verse touches your soul, write it down. Put your verse(s) on an index card. Read them over and over until they are a part of your heart, soul, mind, and strength.

    Psalms 25:4–5; 31:3; 73:24; 139

    Proverb 4:10–13

    Isaiah 42:16; 49:10; 58:11

    Romans 5:3–5

5. Someone once said, "Let go and let God." What are you trying to control? Why?

6. What do you need to surrender today to God's good guidance?

CHAPTER FIVE

Suffering Sojourner

When the pained soul surrenders,
power is displayed.

> "I have never thought a Christian would be
> free of suffering. For our Lord suffered.
> And I have come to believe that he suffered,
> not to save us from suffering, but to teach us
> how to bear suffering. For he knew that
> there is no life without suffering."
>
> (Paton 1948)

Andy seemed to suffer from many ailments. She had lots of aches and pains. She experienced migraine headaches and stomach problems. I wondered what role pain played in her childhood:

> I don't believe I actually experienced excruciating, bona fide, physical pain as a child, but I did learn that in pain, real or not, I had a sense of power.

You see, when I was sick—you know, with the flu or tonsillitis—I was most aware of what the illness offered me. Pain was beneficial because of the special care and consideration I received.

Our family operated within a hierarchy of survival. The person who exhibited abnormal physical symptoms rose to the top of the care ladder. The judge of illness was the mercury-filled thermometer. It was the measuring stick for getting attention, or not. A fever meant I existed; my mom would pay attention to me.

When I was around eight years old, I had a high fever for many days. It was around 106 degrees, or thereabouts. My mom took care of me. I liked that. The doctors did not know what was wrong. Home treatments of aspirin and cool baths didn't help to bring down my temperature, so I was hospitalized. I lay naked on a rubber mat filled with ice water. I remember shaking. I felt alone. In the middle of the night, I looked for my mom. She wasn't there.

Once I got home, I found that I could control the household because I had a mysterious illness. My family paid attention to me. I liked that.

Within a short period of time after arriving home from the hospital, I had a seizure. My panicky mother scooped me up in her arms. She was crying and screaming as she carried me out to the front of the house, yelling for help. I liked being in her arms. I loved being held in my mother's arms.

Pain plays an important role in the work of soul surrender. There is no doubt that one way or another physical, mental, relational, emotional, or spiritual pain is like a megaphone. Pain has the power to get our attention.

Andy discovered that she had power and a sense of control

with her "mysterious illness." She profited by gaining her mother's affection during these "ill" times. Although she believed her illness benefited her as a child, she told me later that she was embarrassed by this realization. She was so desperate for affection that she found illness to be her friend, like a welcomed guest in her home that everyone, especially her mother, greeted with tenderness.

It is interesting to ask people to tell you about their experiences with physical pain. I've noticed that little boys who have had stitches love to tell their stories, especially regarding how many stitches they got. And as far as little girls go, they can be very dramatic. They like to lie down with an ice pack on their injury, or have a foot elevated on a fluffy pillow. Pain provides the opportunity to say, "Hey, pay attention to me."

Have you noticed that women who have experienced labor and the delivery of a baby love to tell their labor stories? I don't believe anything can be more painful than giving birth. For men, the only thing that I have heard of that comes close to childbirth labor pains is passing a kidney stone. Can you imagine ignoring the megaphone of pain from passing a kidney stone or having a baby? Pain is loud and clear. It will not be ignored. It gets our attention.

Pain may be used as God's megaphone. Certainly we can see the purpose of pain as it applies to the journey of soul surrender, in that pain will stop even the strongest people dead in their tracks and bring forth a wailing at God. Pain is like a heavy dose of truth serum. One dose, and we are on our faces, telling all and begging for mercy. Pain can lay us out before the presence and power of God. Peter, a disciple of Christ, heard clearly through God's megaphone the purpose for pain. He said, "Dear friends, do not be surprised at the painful trial you are suffering, as though something strange were happening to you. But rejoice that you participate in the sufferings of Christ, so that you may be overjoyed when his glory is revealed" (1 Peter 4:12-13).

When the pained soul surrenders, the strength of God is displayed. Shelley Chapin, a cancer survivor and author of *Within the Shadow* (1991), speaks about what pain taught her:

> He is teaching me to love, and to cry, and to hunger for righteousness. He is teaching me to count it all loss for the sake of knowing Christ Jesus my Lord. He is teaching me to depend upon Him and to trust His ways. He is teaching me to plant seeds of His love in the lives of others.

Pain is an influential teacher. However, when we are in pain, we are not interested in the lesson, but in relief. We are looking for the answer to our question: "Why do I hurt?" The megaphone of pain pierces our souls. The anguish of the soul drives us to God. Pain may feel as if someone is using a megaphone directly in our ear. We cringe. We want to run and hide from the horrific noise. The noise can drive us away from God. We might even choose to hate God for allowing the pain. Many do.

But pain, if we let it, can actually drive us to God. It was C.S. Lewis, author of *The Problem with Pain* (1940), who called pain "the megaphone of God." This apropos phrase reminds me of pain's potential to place me directly where God wants me.

I have noticed that there are stages that people usually go through when they are in pain, a generalized "pain principle": pain ⤳ panic ⤳ parched ⤳ perspective. When pain hits, most people panic. I like to define panic as fear of the unknown. There is a great deal of fear and confusion about what might be happening. I am always tempted to go to the worst-case scenario with my own pain. For instance, whenever I have a really bad headache, I begin to fear I might have a brain tumor. Do you ever do that? That's panic.

I remember a particular day when I looked into my husband's face and saw intense fear. In a panic-stricken voice he said, "You have to get me to the hospital, now!" There is nothing like a kidney stone to cause a grown man to panic and insist on getting to the hospital, "now!"

Pain leads to panic, and panic causes us to choose a response: fight or flight. Someone who chooses a fight response takes an active approach to the pain. This person hardly stops long enough to feel it. They just get on with the fight until the pain is conquered. Like my husband with the kidney stone—he was interested in one thing: let's get to the hospital and get something to stop this pain.

When people panic, there can also be a flight response, when the soul seeks to run away from pain. I've seen mature men and women carry on a professional conversation as if they have life completely under control one minute and then suddenly jump up and run around in circles shaking their arms wildly when a little bumblebee comes near. They see the bumblebee. They think pain. They panic. They are in flight. The aim of the flight response is to get away from the pain at all costs. Drugs often become the course of action for the flight response. Once my husband was diagnosed with a kidney stone and given pain medication, he was happy. At that point, he gladly chose flight.

When we are in pain, it is natural for us to panic. We want to know why we hurt and what is necessary to stop the hurt. We look for a solution in a bottle of pain medication, a drink, a massage, a new relationship, a spiritual high, or, better yet, an instant miracle. We fear the unknowns of pain. We wonder, "Is there no limit to this pain?" Pain is written into the fabric of life. God allows pain. Pain has a purpose. Yet, in our humanness, we are desperate to cut it out at any cost.

Whether we choose the fight approach or the flight approach, we must understand how pain affects the soul surrender journey. God uses our pain when we cooperate with him. Pain has the powerful potential to propel the soul into surrender.

Martin Luther King Jr. certainly understood the principle of pain. I am sure there were many times that he longed to opt out of the painful call on his life. He said:

> Christianity has always insisted that the cross we bear precedes the crown we wear. To be a Christian one must take up his cross, with all its difficulties and agonizing and tension-packed content, and carry it until that very cross leaves its mark upon us and redeems us to that more excellent way, which comes only through suffering (Yancy 2001).

I am learning to understand my own fears in regard to physical pain. A few years ago I was diagnosed with fibromyalgia. Fibromyalgia syndrome, or FMS, is a very common condition of widespread chronic muscular pain, non-restorative sleep and fatigue. This syndrome gives me the opportunity to bow down to Jesus with my face to the floor and my hands outstretched. In this prone position, I am most comfortable and somewhat pain-free. When I have bad days, I can easily go into a panic mode. I forget that I can actually bow down and find relief. I think it is comical that I am writing a book about surrender, and I find relief from pain in a physically surrendered position.

No one wants to suffer. No one wants to experience pain—physical or otherwise. I have often thought that I deserve to live a pain-free life. Don't you? Yet, if this is our mind-set, we will be disappointed. The aching soul will be in a perpetual argument with God, fighting him or trying to flee from him. If this is our belief—that pain is bad and we should not have any—we will live in a constant state of fear. We are surrendered to fear instead of to God. The suffering soul is too distracted by the fear. The soul becomes parched. The story of Elijah, a prophet of God, demonstrates the idea of a parched soul.

God allowed Elijah to be used to turn the hearts of many people back to God. Although Elijah witnessed the power of God firsthand, he allowed fear to turn him away from God. He feared a wicked woman named Jezebel, who threatened to cause him pain. In fear, he ran for his life. The Bible says, "He came to a broom tree, sat down under it and prayed that he might die. 'I have had enough, Lord,' he said. 'Take my life; I am no better than my ancestors.' Then he lay down under the tree and fell asleep" (1 Kings 19:4b–5).

In his flight, Elijah made a choice: he chose to fear man (or, in this case, a woman) instead of fearing God. Fear thrust him into a flight from God. Although Elijah had profoundly experienced God's power, he now doubted in God's protection. He took life into his own hands and got out of town as fast as he could. You can run, but you cannot hide from the God of the universe.

Elijah was parched. He was tired. He wanted to die. Remember: God didn't leave him. It was Elijah who tried to run from God. Elijah needed to know who the enemy was and when and how to fight. He, like all of us, needs to know who his Savior is and when and how to surrender.

While he slept under the broom tree, an angel of the Lord came to him. The angel said, "Get up and eat, for the journey is too much for you." Elijah got up and ate. He was strengthened. From there he was able to travel forty days and forty nights until he reached Horeb, the mountain of God (1 Kings 19:7–8).

And the word of the Lord came to Elijah saying, "What are you doing here, Elijah?" (1 Kings 19:9b). Elijah explained his plight to God. The Lord said, "Go out and stand on the mountain in the presence of the Lord, for the Lord is about to pass by" (1 Kings 19:11).

And this is my favorite part of this story:

> Then a great and powerful wind tore the
> mountains apart and shattered the rocks before the
> Lord, but the Lord was not in the wind. After the
> wind there was an earthquake, but the Lord was
> not in the earthquake. After the earthquake came

a fire, but the Lord was not in the fire. And after
the fire came a gentle whisper. When Elijah heard
it, he pulled his cloak over his face and went out
and stood at the mouth of the cave. Then a voice
said to him, "What are you doing here, Elijah?"
(1 Kings 19:11–13).

When we have a pained soul we may feel battered, as if a
powerful wind has torn through us. We are broken and barren,
as if rocks have crushed our bones. We fear an earthquake is
threatening to open a hole in the ground to eat us alive. We are
dehydrated, burned up and burned out. God will now speak. He
waits until the pained soul is parched. He knows we are done
fighting him and/or fleeing from him. He now has our full
attention. Now he can be heard. We must be still and listen to
his whisper. His gentle whisper: "My child, tell me, what are you
doing here?" When God asks this question, he isn't looking for
an explanation for your geographical location. He wants to know
why you have given up, like a lifeless ship that has run aground.
Have you become God and concluded that your life is over? Our
souls may be shriveled up, broken, barren, dehydrated, burned
up, and burned out, but for a child of God, life is never over.

In many ways, God is asking, "Did you forget about me?"
"Did you forget that I am the author of your life?" He wants
us to understand that parched places are not the end of life, but
the beginning. He comes to us gently. He gets our attention with
the quietness of his whisper. Through his gentle whisper, we gain
perspective.

At last, our pained souls find relief and a new perspective.
The anguished soul is finally quieted down enough to receive his
mercy. We are suddenly reminded, as A.W. Tozer so eloquently
writes, that:

Mercy is an attribute of God, an infinite and
inexhaustible energy within the divine nature,

which disposes God to be actively compassionate.
Nothing that has occurred or will occur in heaven
or earth or hell can change the tender mercies of
our God. Forever His mercy stands, a boundless,
overwhelming immensity of divine pity and
compassion (Tozer 1978).

Think about this in light of the Apostle Paul's words about
God: "Immense in mercy and with an incredible love, he
embraced us. He took our sin-dead lives and made us alive in
Christ" (Eph. 2:4, The Message).

Pain allows the sojourner the opportunity to see sights he
otherwise would have missed. Without pain, we will speed right
past the rich opportunity to stand upon the mountain in the
presence of the Lord. We don't want to miss out on receiving
more and more of his tender mercy. Let your pain propel you
into his presence.

My physical pains, although simple and not terminal, have
taught me to slow down, be quiet, seize the moment, and
surrender physically to God. Pain has taught me to see that God
is in control of my life. Pain has humbled me and taught me to
depend on God's strength. Pain limits me. It reminds me that
God is limitless. Pain has captured my weaknesses and turned
them into God's mercies. In pain, I have heard his whisper. In
pain, I have received his undying mercy. In pain, I have released
control, and received a display of his power.

Pain teaches us to discover his way as we surrender our way.
We become experts at expressing our emotions and
vulnerabilities to God. At the same time, pain teaches us to trust
him with the very life he has given us.

Many of us try to get out of pain as fast as we can,
so that we can be more "useful" to God. Yet God
reminds us again and again throughout Scripture
that His greatest treasure fills earthen vessels, in

order to show that the transcendent power belongs
to God and not to us. In our weakness, we are
strong. Earthen vessels are God's first choice. Let
God fill you just as you are. Let him touch you
and use you in your fragile and fallible state
(Hansel 1985).

As a suffering sojourner, you must come face-to-face with
your insufficiency until your insufficiency draws you into the
unlimited profusion of God's power. When the pained soul
surrenders, the strength of God is displayed. That is another
golden principle stitched into the fabric of the surrendered soul.

Pain presents the options of either submitting to
the Master Potter's molding/shaping or stiffening
that leads to breaking. Interestingly, even after
stiffening and breaking, God can paste back
together the broken shards, infusing them with
suppleness and life in a way that is even more
glorious than had they never stiffened and
shattered.

Stephen Olsen

GOING FURTHER IN SURRENDER
Chapter Five

1. When you were a child, who paid attention to you? What made you feel cared for?

2. Why does God often wait until we are in the "parched place" before he speaks to us?

3. Are you currently experiencing a pained soul (physically, relationally, emotionally or spiritually)? What is causing the pain and where are you in the process?
   (pain⤳ panic⤳ parched⤳ perspective)

4. How might God want to use this situation to speak his mercy and strength to you?

5. How do these scriptures encourage your pained soul to surrender?

   Lamentations 3:19–24

   2 Corinthians 12:7–10

   1 Peter 4:12–13

6. What other scriptures have encouraged you during a time of suffering?

CHAPTER SIX

A Quenchless Thirst

When the dehydrated soul surrenders,
living water flows.

"My soul thirsts for God, for the living God.
When can I go and meet with God?"

(Psalm 42:2)

Andy expressed that she would like to talk about her marriage—the next phase of her life:

I met this gregarious Jewish boy when I was 16 years old. He loved me at first sight. I thought he was kind of cute, but also kind of annoying. Thus began a rocky relationship. He became my constant companion. Although I was lonely and very needy, at first I rejected his friendship. He pursued me. I would often wonder, "What would a nice Jewish boy want with a gentile girl like me?"

Three years later, I said "yes" to his persistent proposals, and we were married under a chuppah by a rabbi. Bringing our two families together felt weird, like an awkward mixture of water and oil. I wondered how many of our wedding guests whispered the words, "this will never last." I wondered myself.

From the beginning, our marriage was marked with conflict. We struggled with love and intimacy. We struggled with personality differences. We fought over every little thing and every big thing. He wanted six kids; I wasn't sure if I wanted even one kid.

In our relationship, discord was constant. We couldn't find freedom from strife. It felt as if we were in some kind of stronghold and someone or something was seeking to squeeze the life out of us.

Our daughter was born. To my delight, she filled me with a sense of purpose and direction—for a while. I loved being a mom, or at least the idea of being a mom, but I soon found out how impatient I could be. Later, it wasn't enough to be "just a mom." I was restless, discontent and mad.

Then our son was born. We were delighted to have a boy. We were now the perfect American family. We had two kids—a healthy baby boy and a beautiful little girl. We had our own home. At 25, I was able to retire from work and enjoy motherhood. I had everything a girl could ever want, so why did I feel as if I had a thirst that would not be quenched?

Our son was four days old when we moved to our all-new "planned" community in beautiful Southern California. Now I truly had everything: the perfect city, the perfect home, and the perfect little family! My wonderful world was, well, perfect. It was like that paradoxical saying about a dog: "It's so ugly, it's cute!" But for me, the opposite was true: on the outside, my world looked pretty darn cute, but if you could have seen the inside of me, you would have seen something quite desperate—even ugly.

Desperation was woven together with depression; I could hardly get out of bed to care for my infant and my four-year-old daughter. Wrapping up in the covers and sleeping was my escape—the only place I felt any sense of serenity. My husband would deal with our problems by working and playing sports late into the night. I felt abandoned by him. The darkness threatened to swallow me. I would fantasize for hours about a way out. I was so thirsty for something I thought I would die.

In an attempt to try to save myself, I looked to all my external possessions: my husband, my children, my home, my community, and myself, trying to find salvation. There was none to be found, so, like a dried-up water well, I felt useless.

I went to counseling. I was diagnosed with depression. I was depressed about that!

Every move, every thought, and every emotion was overwhelming. As a result of all these problems, I imagined that I was falling into a deep pit that resembled my idea of hell. I began to believe that I had to save myself. I believed that my problems, especially my marriage, were killing me. I believed that I was no good to my husband, myself, or to our children.

In our seventh year of marriage, on Christmas night, I tucked my young children into bed and kissed them good-bye. I opened the front door, stepped out into the darkness and walked away from my children, my husband, our perfect house and our perfectly planned community.

All my attempts to save myself were not working. I walked away from a relationship of idolatry to one of adultery. "Maybe," I thought, "I could find contentment with this man."

An adulterous relationship was my reckless attempt at personal fulfillment. "This new man will satisfy my thirsty soul," I believed. "This relationship will fill me!" I believed that lie as if it were the holy truth, and even found temporary relief from depression.

But, deep down in some tender part of my soul, the longing remained. It would not leave me. Deep down, I wanted to know how to love my husband and how to receive love. I wanted to know how to be loving toward my family. I couldn't put it into words or understand it at the time, but a fuzzy vision was relentlessly taking shape within me. Deep within my thirsty soul, a dried-up riverbed needed to be filled.

We were separated for eight months. I wanted to be together, but just being in my husband's presence was painful. All my pain and anger was directed at him. He was my scapegoat. He was the target of all my anguish, my dissatisfaction, and my insecurity. I blamed him. As crazy as it may sound, we reconciled despite my flip-flop feelings.

Through many more difficult days of searching for answers, I found myself visiting a church.

One day I got up, got dressed, and took the kids and all my tattered baggage to church. I was greeted with kindness and love. The children were joyful over the experience. We began to attend weekly. This little church became a safe place for me. As if it were an artesian spring, I drank in everything I could learn. I kept going week after week so that I could find the source of life, the Living Water I was searching for all along.

Yet there was still that one big secret I carried deep within my heart.

As I reflect on sweet Andy, I realize that she knows something about the thirsty soul and the extremes to which it will go to find water. Her story illustrates the desperation of the thirsty soul, and the depths it will plumb searching for satisfaction.

There is a woman written about in the Bible who experienced the dehydration of her soul (John 4:1–42). Her quenchless thirst actually guided her to enter marriage five times. Like Andy, she was a "gentile" woman.

One particular day, she approached Jacob's well, attempting to divert her burning eyes from the onlookers. Each step was an agonizing and humiliating reminder that the people in her village thought of her as the worst of sinners. Her neighbors would see her approaching and quickly move away, whispering insults just loud enough for her to hear: "Married five times. And now did you know she is living with a man?" She hated going to the well, but she needed water.

There at the well sat a man slumped over, resting. She knew he was a Jew by the clothing he wore. Her humiliation turned to dread. Not only would she experience the scorn of her own people today, she would also have to face what she expected would be the self-righteous superiority of the Jew.

Hoping to avoid any contact, she stepped forward to draw water. She had one thought: "Get the water and get away from him as quickly as possible." She heard his tender request, "Give me a drink." Surprised, she asked, "How come you, a Jew, are asking me, a Samaritan woman, for a drink?" (John 4:9, The Message). Jesus responded to her with kindness. He said, "If you knew the generosity of God and who I am, you would be asking me for a drink, and I would give you fresh, living water" (John 4:10, The Message).

The woman questioned Jesus about his ability to draw water from the well—it appeared he didn't have a vessel to gather water. She went on to suggest that Jesus could not possibly be more capable than Jacob, who gave the well to the Samaritan people in the first place. In essence, she was challenging Jesus' capability to gather or provide any water at all, let alone "living" water.

Jesus began to teach her about the difference between our physical need for water and our spiritual need. He said: "Everyone who drinks this water will get thirsty again and again. Anyone who drinks the water I give will never thirst—not ever. The water I give will be an artesian spring within, gushing fountains of endless life" (John 4:13–14, The Message).

I imagine this woman was interested in the idea presented by Jesus—water that offers endless life. However, Jesus knew what he was after, and it was more than a lofty idea. He presented her with the opportunity to face her life of discontentment. He was leading her in the pursuit of truth. And so he asked her to go and bring her husband back to the well.

She simply responded, "I have no husband." At this point, Jesus let her know that he understood. He reminded her of the five husbands she had previously had, as well as the man she was then living with.

She thought he must be a prophet, and decided to start a theological debate about the proper place to worship. She said, "You Jews insist that Jerusalem is the only place for worship, right?" She was surprised by what he said next:

> But the time is coming—it has, in fact, come—when what you're called will not matter and where you go to worship will not matter. It's who you are and the way you live that count before God. Your worship must engage your spirit in the pursuit of truth. That's the kind of people the Father is out looking for: those who are simply and honestly themselves before him in their worship. God is sheer being itself—Spirit. Those who worship him must do it out of their very being, their spirits, and their true selves, in adoration (John 4:21–24, The Message).

In simple truth, she answered, "I don't know about that. I do know that the Messiah is coming. When he arrives, we'll get the whole story." Jesus answers, "I am he. You don't have to wait any longer or look any further" (John 4:25–26, The Message).

Her heart is pierced by Jesus' words. Somehow she understands that her thirst isn't about well water or about another man. Her thirst is about one man whose name is Jesus. Her thirst can only be satisfied by the gift he offers, that is, living water—eternal life. She dropped her water pot and ran into town to tell all the people about this man. I think it is interesting that she left her pot behind. Symbolically, I see her leaving behind her old life—trying to fill up her soul with men—for a new life, that is, the life that Jesus offers us.

Later in the passage, we see the woman in town proclaiming, "Come see a man who knew all about the things I did, who knows me inside and out. Do you think this could be the Messiah?" (John 4:28–30, The Message).

Jesus stayed with the Samaritan people for two days, and many became believers. The new believers said to the woman "We no longer believe just because of what you said; now we have heard for ourselves, and *we know that this man really is the Savior of the world*" (John 4:42, NIV, emphasis added).

Do you know for sure that Jesus is your Savior? The only one who can truly satisfy your thirsty soul? Can you hear Jesus offering you living water? He offers us living water that is eternal life. His offer will satisfy the dehydrated soul. The word of God confirms this:

> On the last and greatest day of the Feast, Jesus stood and said in a loud voice, "If anyone is thirsty, let him come to me and drink. Whoever believes in me, as the Scripture has said, streams of living water will flow from within him" (John 7:37-38).

GOING FURTHER IN SURRENDER
Chapter Six

1. What was your favorite soda in your teen years? What drink quenches your thirst now?

2. Read John 4:39 and Jeremiah 2:13. What was Jesus getting at by telling the Samaritan woman everything she ever did?

3. In the past, who or what in your life have you hoped would "save" you? Who or what do you look to for salvation now? Who or what will you rely on to save you in the future?

4. If you met Jesus in person right now, what would he say to you?

5. Write out the following scriptures. Reflect on God's word.

    Matthew 5:6

    Psalm 63:5

    Proverb 13:4

    Revelation 7:16–17

    John 7:37–38

6. "When the dehydrated soul surrenders, living water flows." How do you envision this truth working in and through you today?

CHAPTER SEVEN

Life Is Messy

*When the sinful soul surrenders,
forgiveness and freedom are enjoyed.*

*"In him we have redemption through his
blood, the forgiveness of sins, in accordance
with the riches of God's grace that he lavished
on us with all wisdom and understanding."*

(Eph. 1:7–8)

Andy told me her secret:

Shortly after I returned home to my husband and our
children, I got pregnant. I told my husband it was his
child. Together, we decided to abort the baby. I let my
husband believe that he was the father of this baby.
He wasn't. I lied. My sins were spinning out of control.
I felt so disgusted with myself. I had dug a pit so deep
with sin. I was trapped. I felt like I was suffocating. I
wanted to vomit.

Have you ever done something so reckless you wondered how you could possibly undo it? Finding liberation from guilt and shame over our sin is an important daily preparation for soul surrender. We will not be free to live the surrendered life that God calls us to live if we are loaded down with unresolved issues of forgiveness.

Dear, sweet Andy, with her shoulders slumped under the weight of the sins she carried, reminds me of a scene in the 1986 stunning epic movie *The Mission,* directed by Roland Joffe. Mendoza, portrayed by Robert DeNiro, is a slave trader and colonial imperialist who murdered his own brother and seeks penance for his sins by carrying a load tied to his back. He climbs up the rocks of a waterfall with his load of sins weighing him down. It is agonizing to watch.

That gut-wrenching scene reminds me of Andy, who figuratively carried her own 50 pounds of sins in a backpack slung over her shoulders. She had to release this burden to the Lord before she would have the strength and courage to confess the truth to her husband.

God is waiting for us to come to him and confess our sins. He, through the blood shed by Jesus Christ, has already atoned for all sin. There is no price to pay. No work to be done. No load to carry. We need to turn to him in humility and trust that he has paid the price. We do this by putting our faith in Jesus Christ. Stand before God, confess your sins, and hear these beautiful words: "I forgive you my child?" He has removed our sins from us "as far as the east is from the west" (Psalm 103:12).

Andy took her heavy pack off. Trembling, she told her husband the truth about the unborn child. In that moment of confession, she was able to let go of fear, completely trusting God for the outcome. Of course, she didn't feel she deserved to be forgiven by her husband, and even felt that he had every right to divorce her. And then he spoke these words: "Thank you for telling me the truth. I forgive you."

Andy opened her backpack. As she continued the "unpacking," she was surprised to find other heavy burdens. Inside, she found jagged rocks of past pains from childhood abuse. She lifted out smooth river rocks of disappointment. There were bricks of guilt, shame, and fear. Sharp pieces of loss spilled out like broken crystals. There was even a boulder of self-condemnation. She had everything a girl needs to keep her from experiencing freedom. They were before her like lost jewels. Now she understood that her burdens, pain and sins were not her identity. There were no more lies. No more hidden sins. No more secrets from her past. As she laid her burdens down before God, I realized life is messy.

For the first time, I looked at Andy and saw freedom. I gently took each burden, and reverently, I placed them in the bag. With tears in my eyes, I slung the pack over my shoulder. I took her small hand and together we walked forward toward the Cross of Jesus Christ. We walked as one.

You see, dear readers, I am my client Andy. I, Andrea, the counselor and author of this book, am also Andy, the client written about in each chapter. I am the little girl longing for her daddy's love. I am the one who wants so desperately to belong to someone or something bigger than myself. I am the one who has needed to learn the importance of humility. It was me who screamed at God, questioning his guidance and his goodness. And it was me that loved to be sick, so my mom would care for me and hold me. I am also the one who has committed many sins.

I take the backpack of burdens. It is heavy. I walk forward to the cross of Jesus Christ. I hear a still, quiet voice welcoming me. I hear him gently say: "I offer forgiveness for sins, my dear, sweet child. Bring your burden to me. Lay it down. Leave it here at the foot of the cross. I forgive you for every sin you have committed. I have taken on the sins of the world myself. When I was nailed to the cross, it was as if every sin had been nailed to the cross. By holding on to your sins, my child, you're refusing to accept my sacrifice. Every time you condemn yourself, you crucify me all over again. When you refuse to forgive yourself, it is as if you are saying to me, your Savior, that my sacrifice was not good enough for you. Come to me now, and forgive yourself. It is finished. Surrender your sins to me."

I lay the backpack down. I surrender. I journey on.

There is a lady who lives down the street who hangs her laundry out to dry on a clothesline. I don't know why, but I am always fascinated by the array of articles as I drive by. Similarly, through my story, I feel as if I have put all my laundry out for you to take a look at.

I am sharing my story with you because my story is about God and what he is capable of accomplishing in and through a sinful soul like mine. He is more than capable of forgiving the worst of sinners. He is waiting to offer you forgiveness for all your sins.

The issue of forgiveness is another important aspect of soul surrender. Without forgiveness, it is impossible to surrender. It is not easy to forgive. But if we choose to stay trapped with issues of forgiveness, we forfeit the surrendered life. We live without peace. Jesus understood this as he died on the cross for me and for you. It was not easy for him to submit to death on a cross. It is also not easy for us to receive or extend forgiveness. By now I am sure you understand that this is not a book about the easy road to surrender. In forgiveness, we will have to give things up, like pride, bitterness, revenge and anger. In repentance, God liberates our souls and fills us with new proclamations: "I am forgiven. I am liberated. I am at peace."

GOING FURTHER IN SURRENDER
Chapter Seven

1. What is your all-time favorite adventure movie?

2. What adventurous story of yours would you like to share with a child or with your grandchildren? What is the one story you would *not* like to share?

3. Read the Bible story in the Gospel of Luke 7:37–47. Where was Jesus, and what was he doing? Who was the woman and why was she there? What did she do? How did the Pharisee describe the woman? What do you think Jesus' purpose was in telling the parable in verses 41–43?

4. Read Luke 7:44–50. In what ways do you see the sinful woman surrender to Jesus? How did Jesus affirm her? How did he reward her? How important is it to this woman that Jesus loves and forgives her?

5. Which among the following words from Jesus means the most to you right now?

   "For she loved much" (Luke 7:47).

   "But he who has been forgiven little loves little" (Luke 7:47).

   "Your sins are forgiven" (Luke 7:48).

   "Your faith has saved you; go in peace" (Luke 7:50).

6. What is in your backpack today? What are the benefits you receive from carrying your load?

CHAPTER EIGHT

His Glory Manifested

When the faithful soul surrenders,
God is glorified.

"So may glory from defect arise."
(Robert Browning, from "Deaf and Dumb")

Today, I want my life to reflect God's glory. I choose to make known what God has done in and through my life. In that way, I strive to live authentically. I want to be a living testimony, pointing others to the glory of God. It is my heart's desire that God will be glorified as you experience the beauty of surrender. The purpose of soul surrender is this: God is glorified.

This is my story. I was abused as a child. I married young to escape my past and fashion my future. We had two children. I left my husband and my children. We reconciled. I became a Christian. My husband became a Christian. Our children became Christians. After many years of counseling, I went to school to study counseling and began to help others. My husband became a pastor. Recently, we celebrated 35 years of marriage.

Bit by bit, I understand more today about surrender than I did yesterday. I believe I will understand more tomorrow. For now, this is what my life has taught me: I must be willing to surrender all to God, who is the author of my little story, which fits into his Grand Story. I hope your story is unfolding for you in such a way that you are beginning to realize that life is for one purpose—to glorify God. Choosing to glorify God with your life is quite beautiful. It is like watching the sunrise of a new day. You face it, embrace it, and you thank God for it. Surrender to him and let the glory of God shine through.

Today, I am grateful for the opportunities I have been given to work through many painful memories. In my journey of surrendering, God has, indeed, ministered with a healing hand to my weak and wounded soul. It would be a huge error for me to mislead you into thinking that somehow I have reached the goal of surrender. Or, that I have discovered the ten steps to soul surrender. We must remember that surrender is a process, a daily adventure, and a life-long journey. I am joyfully aware that the Lord Jesus Christ has saved me, redeemed me, and healed many of my wounds. I am humbled that he would call me to minister to others who have painful life journeys. Each day in my work, he gently reminds me that I am treading with one of his own on holy ground. Surrender is not about recovery (although recovery may be a piece of surrender). It is a process of discovery.

I continue to have difficult days, struggling with depression and physical discomfort from fibromyalgia. These are precious days, when I am "forced" to surrender and become more aware of his presence again.

An important truth I discovered in writing this book is this: When the soul surrenders, Jesus is glorified. The idea of Jesus being glorified is a recurring theme in my life. Recently, I heard a sermon by John Lamb on that subject. He encouraged us to remember that the goal of all creation is to make God famous. We are created for God's glory (Isa. 43:7). John Lamb went on to say that, in essence, our purpose in life is to make Jesus famous.

Many people desire fame. I don't really know any famous

people. But once, when I was around sixteen years old, I found a little boy unconscious and floating in our apartment complex swimming pool. I jumped in and pulled him out. I gave him mouth-to-mouth resuscitation, and by the time the paramedics came I had revived the little boy. I was written up in our local newspaper as a hero and credited for saving the boy's life. A few years later, I was somehow selected for the Save That Life Award. I was invited to the Beverly Hills Hotel to be the guest of Kentucky Fried Chicken founder Colonel Sanders. He had me tell a bit about my famous day, and then he presented me with the award.

In reality, the Colonel was just a cute old man with a bow tie and a secret chicken recipe. And as for the award, I don't even know where it is. It would be silly of me to live my life proclaiming the glory of the Colonel and the award I received. What isn't silly is for me to seek to proclaim my Lord Jesus Christ, for he is truly the famous one for all eternity.

When the soul surrenders and we choose to live for Jesus Christ, the one who says, "I am the way, the truth and the life" (John 14:6), we represent the glorious one, the real deal. We have the amazing opportunity to proclaim, "I know the famous one!" When the soul surrenders, Jesus is glorified, and we discover that we are not prisoners of the past, trapped in the present or without hope for the future. We are new creations. We are children of God, empowered to be a living testimony pointing to the glory of God.

From the word of God, we know that his glory was present before the earth was created. We know that the whole earth is filled with his glory. We know that we are created for God's glory. We know that we are limited in our time on earth to give him glory. If we choose to place our affections on finite objects, we miss the beautiful opportunity to share in God's glory.

The surrendered soul is in a position to give glory to God. There is no higher purpose than to surrender our all to the Lord

Jesus Christ. There is no deeper fulfillment than to seek his glory daily through surrender.

The unadulterated truth of soul surrender is that it reveals God's glory. When we choose to view surrender as a great romance with the Famous One, we surrender to the marvelous blessings of his glory in and through our lives.

I want my life, my story, to be a living testimony pointing others to the glory of God. I have sought to make known what God has done. It is my soul's desire that he will be glorified in and through this writing. My life continues to teach me the importance of surrender.

I recently spent ten days visiting my mother and father in Bullhead City, Arizona. I watched my once violent father gently put my fragile mother to bed. He is committed to caring for her "until death do us part." As my father was driving me back to the airport shuttle, I felt the Spirit of God nudge me to talk to him, again, about salvation. I decided to cut to the chase. "Dad, last time we talked about your salvation you told me you deserved to go to hell. Where are you at now, that is between heaven and hell?" He responded that he thought he was somewhere in between. He said he was caring for my mother, who has Alzheimer's disease, with tenderness, hoping to do enough good to get into heaven.

Like most people, he believes that he must somehow earn a place in heaven. We think if we just do enough in this world, we earn favor with God. We believe that our kind words and righteous acts guarantee us a place in eternity. God says that our righteous acts are as filthy rags (Isa. 64:6b)

I explained to my father that we are all sinners and fall short of the glory of God (Rom. 3:23). No one deserves to go to heaven—we all deserve hell. That is why Jesus died on the cross. He became the sacrifice for our sins. Because he died on the cross, all of mankind's sins are atoned for. There is only one way to enter heaven, and that is to believe Jesus Christ is the Son of God, who died for our sins so that we can have eternal life. This is God's provision for our sins. It is a gift. We cannot earn it by doing good works. My dad looked at me, smiled and said, "Well, now that is *good news!*"

When we receive his extravagant grace in dying for us, shouldn't his act prompt our extravagant surrender? We want to pour out all that we consider valuable, including our treasures, our talents and our time, and sing, I mean *really* sing, "I Surrender All."

I have discovered a simple, yet beautiful, approach to surrender. God gently calls me to come to him, be still and know that he is God. Once my soul surrenders, I am able to bring glory to his name. It is the glory of the Lord we are after. I can't think of anything more fulfilling. I can't think of a higher purpose than to allow my life to be used to manifest his glory.

When we read through the book of Exodus, we encounter an entire nation moved by God's glory. Moses knew that without the glory of God there would be no hope. David's Psalm of Thanksgiving beautifully explains the glory of God (1 Chron. 16:8–36). The Prophet Isaiah tells us that we were created for God's glory (Isa. 43:7). He proclaims "Holy, Holy, Holy is the Lord Almighty; the whole earth is full of his glory" (Isa. 6:3). Mary sings, "My soul glorifies the Lord" (Luke 1:46). The surrendered soul is in position to be moved by God. Are you willing to be a living testimony pointing to the glory of God? This is our soul purpose!

Longing for his glory reminds me to surrender my agenda. In surrender, I am tenderly brought to a place of releasing self-glory for God's glory. Surrender allows me to let God love me so deeply that the only outcome is for his glory to pour forth.

At the heart of the "good news," we are reminded that grace does not depend on what we have done for God, but rather what

God has done for us. God, himself, deliberately surrenders to the wild, irresistible power of his love for each and every soul.

Famous men like Gandhi, Tolstoy and Dostoyevsky were men who sought surrender, but in the end they hopelessly missed the purpose of surrender, which is to glorify God.

My mom weighs only 79 pounds. She is frail. She wants me to sit with her all the time. I get so antsy sitting. The last day of my visit, I was busy around the kitchen. She was sitting, taking a breathing treatment. She looked at me and said, "Will you just sit down?" I looked back at her and said, "Mom, I just can't sit like you do." She, in her childlike manner, replied, "Well, how do you sit?"

How do I sit?

I sit at the feet of Jesus Christ. Better yet, I fall on my face in awe of him. I wipe his feet with my tears. I seek to surrender my ways for his will. I lie down at the foot of the cross and say, "thank you for your unconditional love, which saved a wretch like me." That is how I sit.

Surrender is a relentless pursuit of authentic faith. The key word here is *authentic*. We must be true to ourselves and embrace the person God created us to be. Surrender may take many different forms. Just as God created each of us uniquely in his image, our surrender is a unique and individual journey.

Surrender cannot become a pharisaical pursuit, or a legalistic exercise. It must be a free-flowing Holy Spirit work—as if a gentle river was flowing directly from God's heart to our souls. He will help each of us find our way.

The Holy Spirit is our internal source and strength for surrender. Our ways must become submitted to his will as we delight in a glorious relationship with Jesus Christ. We are invited to get to know him deeper in the moments of surrender. We are invited to experience the Kingdom of Heaven now. In surrender, we get a glimpse of eternal life. It is something to behold.

Jesus looked toward heaven and prayed:

> Father, the time has come. Glorify your Son, that your Son may glorify you. For you granted him authority over all people that he might give eternal life to all those you have given him. Now this is eternal life: that they may know you, the only true God, and Jesus Christ, whom you have sent. I have brought you glory on earth by completing the work you gave me to do. And now, Father, glorify me in your presence with the glory I had with you before the world began (John 17:1–5).

In surrender, we learn to look inside where the kingdom of God dwells. When we see his glory we realize how short we come up. At that moment, we will want to run from surrender. Instead, it is a glorious opportunity to embrace the full extent of God's amazing grace. In grace, freedom is found. In surrender, I accept God's standard. In grace, I accept Jesus as God's standard for measure.

The last and greatest lesson we must understand about surrender is simply this: we surrender because he is worthy.

> Then I looked and heard the voice of many angels, numbering thousands upon thousands, and ten thousand times ten thousand. They encircled the throne and the living creatures and the elders. In a loud voice they sang: "Worthy is the Lamb, who was slain, to receive power and wealth and wisdom and strength and honor and glory and praise!" (Rev. 5:11–12).

GOING FURTHER IN SURRENDER
Chapter Eight

1. Do you know any famous people? Who? If you could meet a famous person, who would it be? Why?

2. Why do you think so many people desire fame?

3. What does it mean to you to glorify God? In what ways have you done this? How will you glorify him in this moment? How do you hope to glorify him in the future?

4. Do a word study on the word *glory* using the following scriptures. Look for key verses about glory. Write down your thoughts and feelings.

> 1 Chronicles 16:24; 16:28–29; 29:11
>
> Job 40:10
>
> Psalms 3:3; 19:1; 21:5; 26:8; 29:1; 57:5; 66:2; 73:24; 86:9; 96:3
>
> John 11:40; 14:13–14; 15:8; 17:4–5, 22
>
> Acts 7:55
>
> Romans 2:7; 4:20–21; 5:2; 8:17–18; 11:36; 15:17
>
> 2 Corinthians 3:18; 4:15, 17
>
> Colossians 1:27
>
> 1 Thessalonians 2:12
>
> 1 Peter 4:13–14; 5:10
>
> 2 Peter 3:18
>
> Revelation 15:4; 21:23

5. If you could sum up your life with one purpose statement, what would your statement say?

References

Allen, Charles L. 1997. *God's Psychiatry*. Grand Rapids, Mich.: Fleming H. Revell Co.

Allender, Dan and Temper Longman. 1999. *Intimate Allies*. Carol Stream, Ill.: Tyndale House.

Casey, Kathryn. 2002. "Baby Jessica, All Grown Up." http://www.caver.net/j/arch/lhj.html.

Chapin, Shelley. 1991. *Within the Shadow*. Wheaton, Ill.:Victor Books.

Elliot, Elisabeth. 2004. *Gateway to Joy*. "Back to the Bible" broadcast, Oct. 13.

Evely, Louis. 1964. *That Man is You*. Mahwah, N.J.: Newman Press. p. 64.

Hansel, Tim. 1985. Choosing Joy. Elgin, Ill.: David C. Cook Publishing. pp. 122–123.

Joffe, Roland, dir. 1986. *The Mission*. Warner Brothers.

Kimmel, Tim. 1990. *Little House on the Freeway: Help for the Harried Family*. Portland, Ore.: Multnomah Press.

Lewis, C.S. *The Problem with Pain*. 1940. New York: HarperCollins. p. 93.

Lucado, Max. 1999. *The Applause of Heaven*. Nashville, Tenn.: Thomas Nelson. p. 33.

Paton, Alan. 1948. *Cry the Beloved Country*. New York: Simon & Schuster.

Tozer, A.W. 1978. *The Knowledge of the Holy*. New York: Harper & Row. pp. 96–97.

www.jewsforjesus.org. 2004. *Survivor Stories: Finding Hope from an Unlikely Source*. San Francisco: Purple Pomegranate Productions.

Yancy, Philip. 2001. *Soul Survivor*. New York: Doubleday.